# Escape to Japanese Captivity

# Escape to Japanese Captivity

## A Couple's Tragic Ordeal in Sumatra 1942–45

*Written by*
Captain C.O. 'Mick' Jennings
&
Mrs Margery Jennings

Pen & Sword
**MILITARY**
AN IMPRINT OF PEN & SWORD BOOKS LTD.
YORKSHIRE - PHILADELPHIA

First published in Great Britain in 2020 by
Pen & Sword Military
An imprint of
Pen & Sword Books Ltd
Yorkshire – Philadelphia

ISBN 978 1 52678 309 7

Printed and bound in the UK by TJ Books Ltd, Padstow, Cornwall.

Pen & Sword Books Limited incorporates the imprints of Atlas, Archaeology,
Aviation, Discovery, Family History, Fiction, History, Maritime, Military, Military
Classics, Politics, Select, Transport, True Crime, Air World, Frontline Publishing,
Leo Cooper, Remember When, Seaforth Publishing, The Praetorian Press,
Wharncliffe Local History, Wharncliffe Transport, Wharncliffe True Crime and
White Owl.

For a complete list of Pen & Sword titles please contact

PEN & SWORD BOOKS LIMITED
47 Church Street, Barnsley, South Yorkshire, S70 2AS, England
E-mail: enquiries@pen-and-sword.co.uk
Website: www.pen-and-sword.co.uk

Or

PEN AND SWORD BOOKS
1950 Lawrence Rd, Havertown, PA 19083, USA
E-mail: Uspen-and-sword@casematepublishers.com
Website: www.penandswordbooks.com

# Contents

*Maps* ........................................................................................................ vii

*Preface* ..................................................................................................... xiii

*Introduction* ............................................................................................ xv

*Background* ............................................................................................. xvii

**Book One** .............................................................................................. 1

Chapter 1:    When Singapore Fell.............................................................. 3

Chapter 2:    Across Sumatra..................................................................... 7

Chapter 3:    Another Evacuation .............................................................. 15

Chapter 4:    April Fools' Day................................................................... 31

Chapter 5:    The Long Leg ....................................................................... 47

Chapter 6:    Back to the Enemy ............................................................... 59

Chapter 7:    An Ocean Without Shores..................................................... 69

**Book Two** ............................................................................................. 83

Chapter 8:    Hospital................................................................................ 85

Chapter 9:    Heaven Has Curtains ............................................................ 95

Chapter 10:   Palembang 'O' Camp, MULO................................................ 103

Chapter 11:   Hero for a Day...................................................................... 115

Chapter 12:   The Well................................................................................ 125

Chapter 13:   The Guards ........................................................................... 131

Chapter 14:   They're Ours ......................................................................... 133

Chapter 15:   Changi, Singapore ................................................................ 139

**Book Three** .......................................................................................... 145

Margery's Diary ........................................................................................ 147

Philosophy by Margery Jennings ..................................................................167

Imperial War Museum ..................................................................................171

Weight loss ....................................................................................................173

Camps and Dates ..........................................................................................175

*Resources* ......................................................................................................177

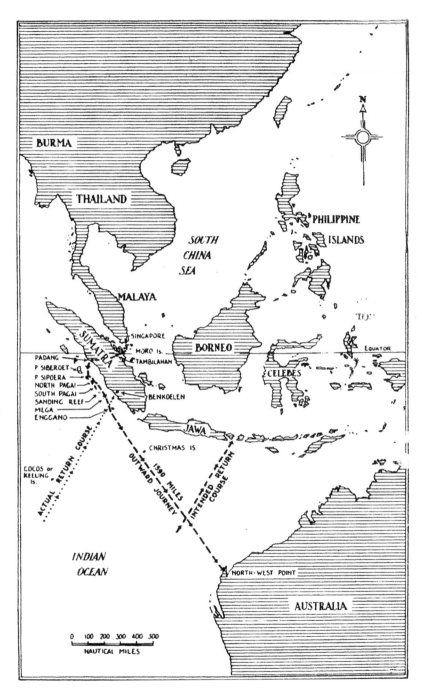

Map 1 – Outward Journey, Intended Return Course, Actual Return Course

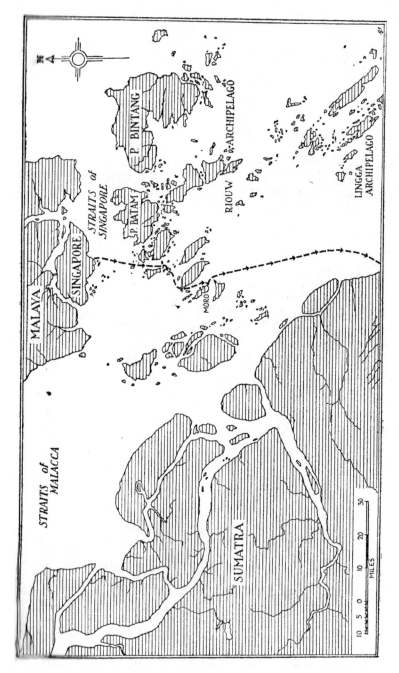

Map 2 – Singapore to Sumatra

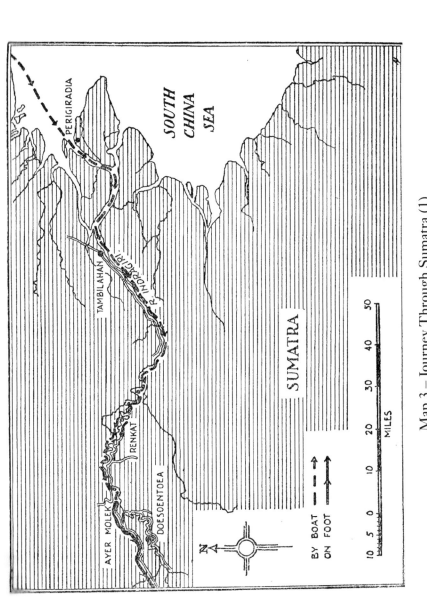

Map 3 – Journey Through Sumatra (1)

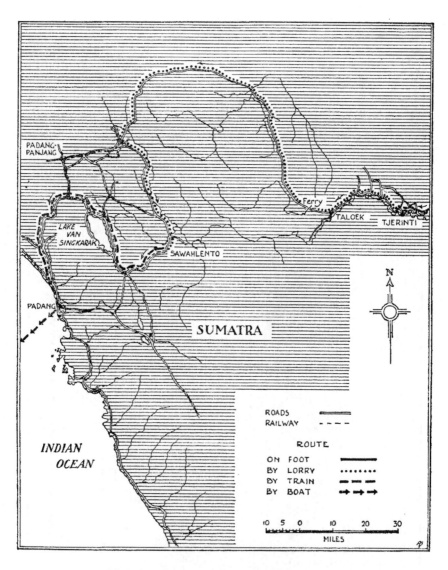

Map 4 – Journey Through Sumatra (2)

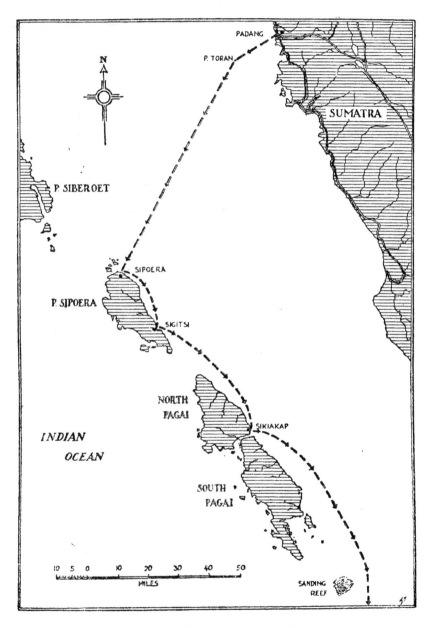

Map 5 – Journey from Sumatra to the Islands

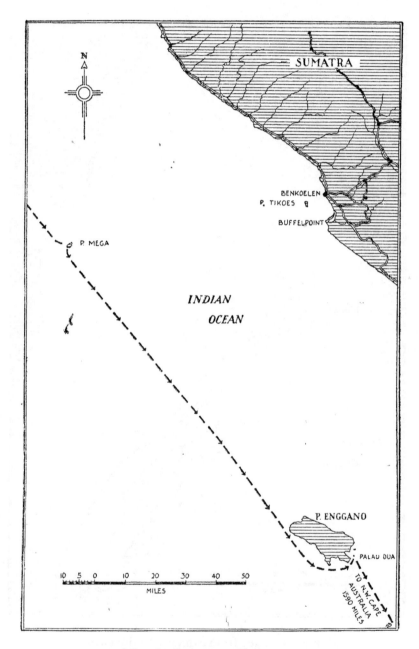

Map 6 – Journey to Enggano

# Preface

It is not the author's intention that *An Ocean Without Shores* be considered a war book. People are sick and tired of the subject, but as this story is not fiction it is necessary that the beginning be where the adventure started – Singapore.

There are no horrors or atrocities to excite the ghoulish mind, but a plain, straightforward tale of the adventures which befell two British soldiers in their attempt to escape from the enemy.

What the chronicle lacks in literary artifice the writer trusts will be balanced by the effort to give the reader a record of the truth, the whole truth and nothing but the truth.

COJ
1950

# Introduction

These books link a husband and wife's story as they left a comfortable life in Singapore to risk danger and death with the city burning behind them, bombed by the Japanese. Mick made a dash for Australia sailing against the trade winds only to land back on Sumatra and go into PoW camp. Margery was captured as she fled in the HMV *Mata Hari* which was bombed in the Java Straits. She went straight into camp, enduring over three years in Sumatra, starving and sick.

**Book 1** describes Mick Jennings' escape from the Japanese after the fall of Singapore, February 1942. Together with other British soldiers he commandeered a local junk and sailed to Sumatra, crossed the island, and from Padang attempted to sail for Australia with Bombardier Jackson Hall in a seventeen-foot dinghy.

**Book 2** is Mick's experience in hospital and PoW camp in Sumatra. He and Margery were able to swap a few letters over the years but never saw each other again. This book takes his story to 1945.

**Book 3** is Margery Jennings' diary which documents her experience fleeing from Singapore, being bombed while sailing south and landing in Sumatra, to spend the rest of the war in various PoW camps on the island. She died of exhaustion in May 1945; the war ended in August. Her diary is kept in the Imperial War Museum in London.

The three books have been condensed and collated by Mick's daughters. *An Ocean Without Shores* was published and is still available online, second-hand, in the full version. *Heaven Has Curtains* was never published; the full version remains in manuscript. *Margery's Diary* has been edited to provide stories of her experience. Again, the full version remains in manuscript form.

# Background

Captain C.O. 'Mick' Jennings, RE, was born in Yorkshire in 1899 to Walter and Edith Jennings. He served with the Royal Engineers in Mesopotamia from 1917 to 1919. He spent the next two years at Sheffield University and then his building and surveying work took him from Yorkshire to the Gold Coast (now Ghana), back to Kent and finally to Malaya, where he became building inspector at Kuala Lumpur in 1935 and later municipal architect. He was again serving with the REs when Singapore fell and his amazing bid for freedom began.

Margery Hellewell grew up in Otley, Yorkshire, with her parents Florence Beaumont Hellewell and Arthur Coates Hellewell, grocer, provision merchant, confectioner and corn merchant. Margery was musical. She became a nurse in the Medical Auxiliary Service in Singapore in the months up to the Japanese invasion.

Margery and Mick had been old family friends in Yorkshire and had written to one another when Mick (then Cyril) went first to the Sudan in 1924 and then to the Gold Coast (Ghana) in 1926 as a surveyor with the colonial government. While on his first tour of duty in West Africa, he began to think of marriage. It was always difficult to find an English wife from such a distance and indeed being married was often impossible until you reached a certain age, perhaps 30.

In the Sudan he had lived in the bush in a tent. He slept with his rifle at his side and both flaps of the tent left open so that if a lion walked in it could walk straight out the other end with a bit of luck. In the Gold Coast he would be away surveying with a party of Ghanaians for three weeks at a time.

Now in Accra, he had a government bungalow, drove a Riley and could accommodate a wife. He made a list of all the girls he knew back in the UK. Margery Hellewell had written regularly and rather opened her heart to him. Perhaps she should be the one. He probably wrote to her to that effect. Anyway, they were married on his first long leave in England.

Mick's wedding present to her was an upright double-strength piano which they took to Accra. They were given a little wire-haired fox terrier they called Smut because he rolled in the coal under the house one day. He came to Africa too as company for Margery.

That first eighteen months in West Africa must have been a difficult and often lonely time for Margery with Mick away so much. Consequently, she concentrated on her piano playing and became an accomplished musician. This proved to be a boon later in prisoner-of-war camp in Sumatra where music featured strongly. Both Mick and Margery had lovely voices; Mick used to sing on the radio in its fledgling state in Malaya.

They had decided not to have children because they lived overseas in conditions with limited healthcare and schools. Children would have kept Margery busy, but perhaps it was just as well in the long run.

In 1935 Mick became Town Board building inspector in Kuala Lumpur. Margery adapted well to Malaya, learning Malay, playing the organ in the church and later nursing as the war came closer.

Mick's hobby was motor racing his many MGs, which is where his nickname came from because he used to have a Mickey Mouse badge on the front fender of his car. Perhaps it brought him luck.

It was hard for them to realize the growing threat of the Japanese invasion, believing in the might of the British Forces and the impregnability of Singapore. The diary begins with Margery playing at church services and for weddings and doing her nursing duty. Mick re-joined the Royal Engineers (he had fought in the Great War) and implemented the scorched earth policy, destroying bridges to halt the Japanese advance, and smashing bottles of whisky to deny the enemy the chance of getting unpleasant. Even though people were escaping in February 1942, many wanted to stay and uphold the cause, especially the nurses. Only at the last minute did Mick and Mr Hinch decide the ladies should leave.

For the next three years, Margery's diary records the daily misery of camp life and her longing to be back in a normal world with Mick. As the prisoners' health eroded with the poor food and many diseases, the deaths increased until a third of the women succumbed. She kept her faith and looked to the skies for freedom and beauty.

# BOOK ONE

## Chapter 1

# When Singapore Fell

'Did you say *destroying* bottles of booze, sir?' asked a tubby sergeant whose blue eyes stared incredulously from an unshaven face. I replied that was correct, which left that worthy NCO completely speechless. A moment later, after a deep breath, he blurted out, 'Do you mean *smashing* bottles of whisky, sir?' I confirmed the order and told him to get the men and hurry up. The happiest sergeant in the British Army gave me a particularly enthusiastic 'Verree good, sir', and let out a roar which soon had troops popping out from all kinds of strange places where they were taking cover from Japanese mortar fire.

It was the fourteenth day of February 1942 and early that morning Lieutenant Colonel Meade, RE, had instructed me to proceed to the Borneo Company's godown [warehouse] in Magazine Road and destroy 30,000 bottles of whisky, brandy, gin and champagne, adding that the Japs were very nasty little men when they were drunk. Patently the military position on the Island was changing hourly and it was evident our position was rapidly deteriorating.

Many fume-laden hours later I went to report to Lieutenant Colonel Meade that the task was completed and ask what the next job might be. Before he could reply, the telephone started ringing, and a captain answered the phone with some curt grunts. Turning to Colonel Meade he said, 'Lieutenant X at the water post in Havelock Road has ordered his men to surrender, sir.' I began making wild guesses about my next job, when Colonel Meade said, 'Get Fort Canning on the line,' and we waited silently for the connection to be made. When this was done, Colonel Meade mentioned Havelock Road and asked for instructions. He paused to listen, then said, 'Very well, in half an hour.'

We waited and waited, not a single word said between the three of us. Cigarette ends littered the floor at my feet. It was obvious something momentous was afoot and the OC knew much more than he cared to say. It was 5.25 pm when the phone rang again. The information transformed Colonel Meade into an old man. He put the receiver down and, turning to me heavily, said, 'Jennings, please get the men in a circle. I want to speak to them.'

Clambering up the dugout steps, I gathered the troops and a few minutes later he stood with his men around him and said:

'Gentlemen, today at 4.30 pm the British Commander-in-Chief surrendered unconditionally to the Japanese Commander-in-Chief. You are now at liberty to try to escape or to stay, as you desire; but if you go I am to advise that you go in uniform otherwise, if captured, you may be shot as spies. That is all.'

There are moments in a person's life which can never be forgotten. Moments of beauty, love or achievement, hate or hopelessness, and moments of breathtaking amazement and disbelief. Although it had been clear for the past week there could be no other ending than this, the shock of being told the end had come held us silent and still, staring at the man we had come to love and respect, waiting until he should break the spell which had descended.

A shell bursting closer than usual brought us back to reality and reminded us that if we wanted to make a bid for freedom even minutes were important. I went up to Colonel Meade, saluted, shook hands and said goodbye. I had made up my mind to try to escape. How, I knew not but I hoped the opportunity would present itself. The great thing was not to be captured, and an intense desire for freedom seized me. Could it be done? Was it too late? My wife had left a few days earlier on the *Mata Hari* and I trusted she was well on her way.

Everyone seemed to be of the same mind and rushed to cars and lorries. Only the sea could offer the chance of escape and going up to my car I threw out the bag which contained all the personal belongings that remained to me. It was no good being hampered with a heavy suitcase when attempting to escape. In convoy with other cars, some twenty-seven of us retraced our way down Tanglin Hill. On either side of the road were our silent guns and standing by them were the bewildered gunners who had fought so splendidly, idly watching our procession of cars. It was evident they had not yet been told of the capitulation. It was a heartbreaking sight which made the lump already in my throat much larger. It seemed shameful to be creeping away, but we had been given a chance of escaping and were naturally trying to make the best of the opportunity.

What chaos the wharf presented! Frustrated troops could be observed hurrying from one boat to another in the hope of finding something, any-thing, in which to get away. Two RAF launches appeared to be the focal point of hope, judging from the crowd. They were afloat and apparently undamaged so towards them we made haste with more speed than dignity. Here and there military police were vainly trying to stop men from what appeared to be wholesale desertion.

We boarded the already overcrowded RAF launches and inspected the engines. The injector plugs were missing so it was no use wasting any further time on them. Coming on deck I peered over the side and noticed a small dinghy with seven men in it. Here was the chance I was looking for. Handing my Tommy gun and haversack containing food and cigarettes to an officer, I told him I would bring the boat back, and leapt over the side of the launch into the boat just as the occupants were attempting to push off. I scrambled forward and to someone's instructions we took off our tin hats and paddled for all we were worth as the light was rapidly failing. Some 500 yards seaward lay the breakwater which divided the inner roads from the open sea. It was deep twilight by the time we reached it. We had got off the island, but only just.

Moving eastwards along the breakwater, we came to a point opposite the useless RAF launches, when a lone soldier appeared and asked if we knew where fresh water could be obtained. One of our party gave him a drink, after which he informed us that he belonged to another party of troops a short distance away. A minute or two later we came upon seventeen other men who had obtained another small dinghy, on the seaward side of the breakwater. We banded together, making a party of twenty-five in all.

In this group of men I met Captain Crawley, RA, who was trying to get some sort of organization into this escaping business, and the dinghy made several trips to one of the *tongkangs* [junks]. On one *tongkang* we came upon a small certificate fastened to the bulkhead, which informed us that we were on the *Hiap Hin* of 135 tons registered berth, a sound, solid and seaworthy craft. The water tanks were full and in the hold were six bags of rice. We crept about in the darkness of our unfamiliar new home but found nothing else that was edible. We did, however, find some clothes which had belonged to the previous crew. The knowledge that the vessel was empty of cargo and therefore riding high in the water gladdened our hearts for we knew that whatever course we laid, we had to sail through our own minefield. Captain Crawley was nominated skipper and I, one of the ship's officers. Though we had plenty of rice, we dared not light a fire and a drink of water took the place of supper. No one minded this, for we were all too excited to eat and eager to prepare the vessel for sea. At precisely 4 am on 16 February 1942, we weighed anchor, hoisted sail and set course for Sumatra.

At 6 am I was wakened to take my turn on watch and in the breaking light I noticed a small sail in the near distance. A little while later the boat tacked and downed sail right in our tracks. As we altered course to pass by, the stranger hoisted sail again and came alongside. He shouted in Malay that anyone could tell we were escaping soldiers because we had the sail inside out! There was a roar of laughter from our crew when the message was interpreted. We threw a rope to the fisherman and he came aboard and helped us to rectify our tell-tale error.

Our visitor advised us to go to Maru Island, where food could be obtained. After explicit directions on how to recognise this haven from the maze of islands surrounding us, he took his leave, wishing us 'Selamat jalan' [safe journey]. Clambering back into his small craft, he sailed away to await any other escapers and hand on to them his most valuable information.

After several days of sailing we dropped anchor at Maru Island where Captain Walker welcomed our party and told us we had made contact with an official organisation for aiding escapers. As each ship with escaping troops aboard arrived at Maru Island, it left an officer to relieve the one left by the preceding boat, thereby giving that officer who had stayed behind to issue stores and give sailing directions his chance to try and escape. We, in fact, left three people behind at their own request. This gave Captain Walker the opportunity to come with us. Cases of food were manhandled down the hillside and into dinghies and then loaded on the *Hiap Hin*. There were some 130 men on Maru whom we proposed to take with us. They were consequently pressed into service to help in provisioning the ship.

All through the night our *tongkang* sailed on, now in more open sea, and early the following morning we sighted the sunken junk, one of our landmarks, under the lee of an island and accordingly altered our course. By this time, we considered ourselves seasoned deep-sea sailors and had every confidence in Crawley's ability to reach Sumatra. That same evening, we came abreast of the fishing *pagar* [fence] and most of the night was spent talking and guessing the time we should sight our next turning point, as we knew that the land we would then be looking at was Sumatra, which held all our hopes of escape.

## Chapter 2

# Across Sumatra

After many days of travel on small boats up the rivers, on foot and by truck and train across Sumatra, we reached Padang. Padang station was a small, isolated brick building set down in the middle of a plain and connected to the town by a metalled road. I can imagine it would be a miserable spot on a rainy day but to us escapers the place was paradise. To the west could be seen the town proper and we were keen to get there to learn the latest news regarding shipping. All personnel, both civilian and military, eagerly left the coaches and lined up on the road facing the booking office.

We were told how to find the rendezvous and I gave the order to march. Leaving the station, we walked two miles through the town to a school which had been allocated to us. After seeing my party settled in a classroom and making arrangements for food, I went to the Endraach Club, where Lieutenant Colonel Warren, RM (OC British Personnel, Padang), gave the officers a cheerful pep talk officially welcoming us to Padang. The colonel appeared optimistic about our chances of escape and indicated all we had to do was wait for a destroyer to take us away. The whole business seemed simplicity itself.

I returned to the school and told the party what Colonel Warren had said. I asked Bombardier Jackson Hall, whom I had befriended during our time together on the *Hiap Hin* if he would come for a walk, and when we were alone gave him my private opinion regarding our chance of escape, pointing out everything had been made to look so simple that it was, in fact, too simple. It was my intention to find the home of the British Consul to glean any further information.

Entering the office, we were met by the vice-consul, Mr Levison. We received a jolt when he gave us the tragic news that signals could not be sent as, following instructions, he had destroyed the code book. He said the last destroyer had left Padang only two days previously, so there was still a chance of further ships coming to our rescue.

One redeeming feature of this visit was that we had got the truth and the truth did not coincide with the pep talk. Mr Levison produced lists of

British civilians who had already passed through Padang but there was no record of my wife.

Leaving the consul's office, we turned to look at his residence. In the windless afternoon hung the Union Jack, still and lifeless, an ill omen. We hurried away to find more cheerful things to look at.

The following day, 10 March, several of us walked down to the sea where on a lovely sandy beach, huge breakers were rolling in. Looking towards the distant horizon, Hall turned to me and said, 'See anything, Skipper?'

I replied, 'No, Jack. I was just thinking the ocean is rather like a railway line which connects us with freedom. There is our line of communication and all we want is a boat, so I suggest we go and find one.'

Scouting around, we came to a small river where some craft were lying at anchor. Opposite were shipping offices where we might get help. Every chance had to be explored. Entering one of the offices I was surprised to see the desks were occupied mostly by Europeans and business was being carried on as usual. Asking about getting passages on their ships, even if only to the islands a hundred miles away, I was told the small craft (about 80 tons) which were tied up alongside the riverbank were being kept for the Japanese for the transportation of rice to the islands. Something must be wrong, I thought. Perhaps the individual had misunderstood my questions. So I asked again and was curtly told not to waste their time. When the Japanese arrived, they would carry on with their work as before, but for the benefit of the enemy. My party had edged through the door and heard everything. They stared at one another disbelievingly.

We wandered back to our billets and while the men were still saying unkind things about 'Allies' I went to the Endraach Club to listen to another pep talk. Over 100 British officers were informed that the Dutch commander had decided to declare Padang an open city. I leave the reader to judge what kind of remarks we made.

The British personnel included many sailors who had survived the sinking of the *Repulse* and *Prince of Wales* and were capable of manning ships far larger than the small craft we had seen in the river. One party set off to investigate the possibilities of obtaining a vessel. These men did in fact board a ship, only to be ordered off by Dutch sailors at the point of a revolver. Even the machine guns on the breakwater were trained on them, compelling them to retire.

In orders the following day, 12 March, the harbour and river were placed out of bounds to all British troops. The Dutch were playing a forcing two game [a bridge term meaning forcing the game], which meant our efforts to escape were being scotched. Schemes for getting away were made and as quickly discarded. No one believed we would just be abandoned, even when low-flying Japanese reconnaissance aircraft crossed the town without a shot being fired. Hopes still lingered of being rescued by destroyers during the hours of darkness. The troops received a payment of five guilders each, enabling them to buy extra food and cigarettes. This money had the desired effect of keeping them quiet. Not once during all those depressing days did I see any brawling or troublemaking. Keenness to get away was the uppermost thought in everyone's mind.

The pep talk to the officers on 13 March was the most pessimistic I ever had the misfortune to listen to. Colonel Warren had no smiles as we crowded round the table at which sat Colonel Dillon and a Dutch officer. Colonel Warren (unnecessarily we thought, since Padang had been declared an open city) began by explaining that the Dutch commander was prepared to surrender to the Japanese but we were all surprised when he said that he (Colonel Warren) would work under the Dutch commander, giving us his word of honour not to try to escape. This ghastly news produced a very gloomy effect. Frustration was evident as the officers, knowing there was no more to be said, made their solemn way out of the building.

Reaching the verandah, I heard a voice calling my name and turning around saw Colonel Dillon beckoning me. Walking to a quiet spot, he said, 'Jennings, if that ship doesn't come tonight, it looks like another Singapore.' I thanked him for his confidence. I had been tipped that we were almost as good as in the bag and again it was every man for himself. I went back to the school, turning over in my mind all we had gone through to get away from Singapore. My thoughts could be printed, but never published.

After supper, I was given more money for the troops by a lieutenant MRNVR [Malayan Royal Navy Volunteer Reserve], who suggested they not be paid until the following night. I thought this was a bit fishy, as that officer had previously acted as paymaster. Why should I be asked to pay them? Not that I minded, but the request seemed peculiar. Everyone's wits were sharpened. One party began watching another party, trying to glean the latest escape plans. This resulted in a crop of stupid rumours. There was only one topic of conversation, of course, and that was escape. Would the ship come? That question began to sear my soul, as I dared not betray Colonel Dillon's confidence and yet I did not wish to raise false hopes for my companions' sake. I gave them my opinion that it would be best if they tried to get away as I myself intended. In nearly every haversack sat a school atlas, which showed in detail the countries comprising the NEI [Netherland East Indies] and the islands off the western seaboard of Sumatra.

In Padang were a thousand British people, men, women and children with hope in their eyes, who could not keep away from the sea. All that was required was a ship and there were sufficient vessels in the harbour and river to get everyone away. The situation seemed monstrous and absurd, particularly as we had men able and only too willing to man the ships. It seemed as though we could feel the Japanese net closing in on us and our Allies bursting with laughter, but we were determined not to sit down and be taken. It struck us as fantastic that we should be expected to wait for the inevitable to happen. We wanted action and the only way we could keep busy was by preparing our escape kit. Parties of men went into town searching the marketplace for knives, tinned food and other useful gear. That night, maps, compasses, water bottles and food were gathered and guarded carefully.

When morning came on 14 March, schemes for getting away from Padang overwhelmed even food. One could feel zero hour was not far away. Some men were for going native. Others even now suggested retracing their steps across Sumatra. But how could a fellow get back into the Indian Ocean, assuming he was lucky enough to get a boat on the Indragiri River? He would have to sail her back through the Japanese lines. The point was, where could we get a boat? After hectic discussion, the answer came in a flash. Why stay in Padang?

The 1,200-mile-long island of Sumatra is almost exactly bisected by the equator with Padang, the capital, a few miles inside the southern hemisphere. Padang was only one tiny spot on the western seaboard, and we would get away from the stupid control exercised there. How far away were the Japanese? We knew they were closing in from both north and south. They might be only ten miles from Padang or even five. Perhaps we would run into them and be captured at once. All this had to be risked. So parties searched in both directions. Some were fortunate enough to get boats. Others did not because they had no money and, still retaining a sense of decency, did not stoop to stealing a boat which they could easily have done.

Disappointed troops, having spent the whole day searching for suitable boats, returned to the school billet for their evening meal. Their morale was on a steep downward curve and the pay I issued did little to cheer them.

That evening I visited the town hall where most of the British women were accommodated. On the first floor a kind of welfare organisation was in operation and they had the unpleasant task of publishing lists of missing, killed and drowned persons, prepared from information supplied by survivors. As far as my personal worry was concerned, my wife, I drew a blank and left this unhappy building where mercy was being so generously dispensed.

I went to the Endraach Club for what was to be my last pep talk. Quite a few of the officers were missing, including Colonel Dillon and the RNVR paymaster-lieutenant, which was why I had been asked to pay the men. They had apparently been lucky in getting boats. The authorities now realised that neither we nor the troops could be bluffed any longer.

For payment, the men had received five guilders and the officers ten; the money was invariably pooled among three or four individuals. It was generally accepted that small parties would stand a much better chance of getting away than large ones. My own party was reduced to four men and we were already equipped with what we considered the essential escape gear, the goods purchased from our pooled fund. Later we found we had forgotten the most essential things but, in our ignorance, we had a confidence that nothing could shake. In retrospect this attitude appears amusing, as so far we had not procured the very first essential, a boat!

There was a tenseness in the night air and talk of escape ceased. Yet, as tired heads began to nod, it seemed as if the very atmosphere was shouting, 'Escape! Escape!' During the early hours, small groups of men stole quietly out on their desperate bid for freedom. A silent wish 'Good luck and may you make it' came from us who lay awake.

To the north, east and south lay impenetrable jungle and mountain ranges; to the west, thousands of miles of ocean. Our companions had made their choice and were entering upon an adventure which might bring them success but the odds were a million to one against. Tomorrow I too would be bucking against the same odds. Clutching my escape gear more tightly, I fell asleep.

March 15 dawned and over breakfast we remembered those comrades in Singapore who had now been prisoners of war for exactly one month. What aeons of time had passed since that fatal day! Feeling the need for a little quiet thought, I went for a stroll, and on my return met a gentleman in Salvation Army uniform near the school. He hailed me cheerfully, introducing himself as Major Mepham. He told me, among other interesting things, that he was Canadian and, with his wife, was in charge of a hospital, which I subsequently found was doing wonderful work for our sick and wounded. He was not permitted to preach the gospel in Sumatra, as this was contrary to Dutch law, but he could preach on the islands to the west. I was not interested in preaching, but I did want some first-hand information about those islands. Naturally I grilled him thoroughly and learned about the Mentawai people, who were Christians and would help us if we ever got there. This was important information and would greatly interest the troops.

The major then asked me if I thought the boys would like a little service and I said they would be delighted (with tongue in cheek) as everyone in the school without exception was interested in one subject only: how to get away from Padang. The padre seemed pleased and arranged to come to our quarters in the afternoon.

Back in the billet, I mentioned having met a Salvation Army padre who knew the islands well. The eyes of the men shone with excitement as I told them what I had heard, adding the major would be coming around in the afternoon to give us a short service. There were a few groans and the major and his service were promptly forgotten, for a new word had entered the men's vocabulary: Mentawai. Maps were produced and sure enough, printed near some islands named Pagai North and Pagai South, were the words, 'Mentawai Group'.

Billeted in the school were about 250 men from all the branches of the British fighting services who, if not out searching for boats, were on the open verandahs of the building, either eating or in small groups planning their getaway. The midday meal was finished, and tea was being prepared by the naval ratings in the galley when, as arranged, the major came walking down the road to be confronted by the solemn faces of men who couldn't care less about singing hymns. This padre was a tough little fellow and did not mind the snubbing, which unwittingly drew me to him. With a knowing smile which told me he knew what we were thinking, he opened a small hymnbook and to half a dozen men (I had to be there) began singing a well-known hymn in which we half-heartedly joined. At the end of the first song he turned over the pages of his book and with a smile, started on another hymn. He hardly gave us time to get our second wind. We were up against something tougher than we had bargained for. This fellow was going to make us sing and like it.

The power of music began to work and in ones and twos the soldiers began to gather round the man who would not be snubbed. 'With a twinkle in his eyes he said, 'If you boys don't mind, I'd like to say a few words.' He did and very beautiful and encouraging words they were. It seemed to dawn on most of the troops that this man was not just blethering to please us. He too was in the trap. In other words, he was one of us, with us. The prayer ended with 'The Lord is my shepherd, I shall not want'. The major then led us in another hymn, which completed his small service, or at least that was what he said. Most of the troops were standing around by this time and the wire fence was lined with natives who had been listening to the hymn singing. I suppose they were wondering what on earth we had to sing about, when in a day or so we would be slaves of the victorious Japanese.

The playground of red laterite, bare and uninviting except for a small part occupied by the crowd of sullen-faced fighting troops next to the open verandah, the little padre facing them, and the gazing natives, all seemed unnatural in a coating of gold from the westering sun. The hymn had just finished and, uncertain what was to come next, complete silence reigned, with every eye on the major. The padre started to speak with his peculiar intonation these memorable words: 'Boys, before I go, let us sing that grand hymn, "Land of Hope and Glory".' The words came out clear and crisp. Those men to whom this service had been nothing but a damned nuisance were jerked off their seats as if something had stung them. It was magic, the magic of patriotism. Our little friend gave us the key in the opening word, 'Dear Land of Hope...' and in a clear tenor voice he sang the verse practically as a solo. Some of us could not sing, simply because we would have choked. Others did not know the words. A few rough hands were wiped across eyes, while others blew red noses. As the verse ended, there was a split second of silence followed by a mighty roar: 'Land of Hope and Glory'. I thought I knew something of the power of music, but this was amazing. With a lump in my throat and misty eyes, I pulled back my shoulders like everyone there, and bellowed fortissimo the greatest British song ever written. The crowds of wondering natives listened to words they did not understand, but they did comprehend that 'Mother of the Free' had a very special significance for the singers as they saw the effect on men who, five minutes previously, had sat with hunched shoulders and hopeless faces. Here were the same men but with a different spirit, swung from despair to hope by the tremendous meaning contained in that song, men who were now standing proudly with shining eyes, transformed from a broken army to a fighting force.

As the padre left us, we gave him three cheers that might have been heard by the Japanese and I believe, as he raised his hat to us, that tough little man had a suspicion of moisture about his eyes too. On behalf of my comrades, for that one inspiring moment, wherever you are, Major, I salute you.

## Chapter 3

# Another Evacuation

While working in Fort Canning, Singapore, in 1940, I had met Captain James Thorlby, RE, and was surprised and pleased when at about five o'clock one evening he came to the school and told me he had procured a boat through the services of a Penang Eurasian and would I come with him. He said his party, besides himself, were:

Major Rowles, chaplain
The Eurasian boy (I never knew his name)
Corporal Good, Cambridge Regiment
Private Green, Sherwood Foresters
Private Birch, Recce Corps

As his party numbered six, I asked about the size of the boat. He thought it was only small, but as he had never seen it he could only give second-hand information. I spoke to the Eurasian, who seemed hazy about the length and breadth, but I gleaned it was a sizable boat and of quite decent length. Most of my companions did not relish the idea of attempting to cross a hundred miles of open sea in a boat full of amateur sailors. It was obvious that the willing members of Party 14, plus Thorlby's six, could not be accommodated in a craft of 'quite decent length', even though the people who had fallen out of the scheme made selection much easier. Finally, my party consisted of the following:

Warrant Officer MacLaren, RASC
Sergeant Anderson, Anti-Tank Regiment, RA
Bombardier J. Hall, Anti-Tank Regiment, RA
and myself

It was arranged that while Thorlby returned to his billet to collect the padre and the others, we should acquire *gharries* [horse-drawn cabs] and wait for them at a rendezvous some distance from the school. Gathering our escape kit, we made a rapid check of our compasses, maps, food, water bottles, etc., and saying goodbye to our old party, we walked to the main street where we hired the gharries and soon met four of Thorlby's company.

Falling in with Thorlby's party was sheer luck for us, as up to the time when he approached me, all our efforts to find a boat had been in vain, though we had arranged to meet two Indonesians who said they could get a boat for us that night. That, of course, was now unnecessary as here we were on the road and once again journeying into the unknown in search of freedom.

Twenty minutes later our guide ordered the driver to stop. We quickly dismounted from the ancient vehicle and waited for the others to catch up. After paying the drivers, we turned into the lane and 200 yards distant entered a *kampong* [village] on the seashore. Some time elapsed before we found the Indonesian who had agreed to sell his boat, which we did not get as easily as I had imagined. A crowd of about twenty Indonesians tried to persuade the owner not to let us have the boat, suggesting there would be dire consequences when the Japanese arrived. A precious half hour was spent arguing before the boat became our property. The essential items were then stowed and the padre (Major Rowles) pulled out a roll of notes and handed 90 guilders to the seller. The man asked for a receipt but why it was necessary I fail to understand. If anyone needed a receipt it was us to prove we had not stolen the boat.

The dugout canoe was twenty-six feet long and two feet in the beam. One glance convinced Sergeant Anderson that it was unsafe for a sea voyage and saying goodbye, he turned back to Padang. Watching his lone, khaki-clad figure making its way through the group of hostile villagers, I felt a mixture of pleasure and remorse; pleasure because the lack of weight would give the rest of us a better chance and remorse because he looked so lonely and was deliberately renouncing his last chance of freedom.

We turned to the immediate job of pushing our frail link with freedom over 200 feet of sand to the sea. It was almost dark when the bow of the canoe rested in the shallows. The mast was then stepped and one native, kindlier disposed than the rest, jumped on the high curved prow and helped us to claw off the land, a difficult task owing to the breakers.

There were ten of us in the boat, including the local man and a quantity of water, so we had a freeboard of only two inches. It was evident the boat was grossly overloaded, and it was only a matter of time before the most nervous or most sensible (according to the way you look at it) tried to get back to the beach. When we were clear of the breakers, the man pointed to a reef a few miles out to sea and told us to keep well north of it. Then, wishing us 'Selamat jalan', he dived into the sea. His going broke the spell. It was evident our Eurasian friend was uncomfortable. He obviously thought he would be safer on shore because, he explained, with his knowledge of the language he could easily go native. We wished him well.

The sail was up and drawing nicely. The occasional small wave slapped over the gunwale, but we were too busy managing the boat to notice such things. She was afloat and getting further from land every minute. MacLaren took off his boots and tied them together, asking if we would put back to shore as he thought we hadn't a chance with so many people. The small craft was brought round in a big circle to the seaward edge of the breakers and, slinging his boots round his neck, MacLaren gave a quiet 'Cheerio chaps' and dived over the side. The last time we saw him he was swimming powerfully towards the distant lights beyond the breakers. The remaining seven of us turned our faces resolutely from the shore and set course south of an atoll about fifteen miles distant upon which we had taken a bearing before the light failed.

Three and a half hours after leaving Sumatra we sighted the atoll on our port beam and steered directly for it. Here our seamanship was put to a severe test as we tried to ride the breakers surrounding the island. Water poured into the boat and when it had risen to within a few inches of the gunwale and foundering seemed certain, we felt the grinding on the coral of our first landing. From the shore the breakers looked enormous and we wondered how we were going to get through them into deep water again. Why we wanted to land on Pulau Toran I do not know. There was no need other than heavy rain which made everyone uncomfortable. After riding the breakers, we were all much wetter than we had been before, as was every item of equipment we possessed.

Pulling the boat up the beach we scouted around and about a quarter of a mile away found a dilapidated hut sitting among the coconut palms. This was luck indeed and at the side of the hut away from Padang we made a small fire and had a welcome brew of tea. Complimenting ourselves upon the successful first landing, we chatted awhile and one by one fell asleep. So ended 15 March 1942, one month after the fall of Singapore.

We were up before dawn and began a tour of our temporary domain. There seemed to be something missing which I could not place and, mentioning this to the others, found they had the same feeling. In the evening our sleep had been disturbed by the pounding breakers, which had now disappeared.

We searched for fresh water, as no one would have built a hut there if water was not available, and a few minutes later discovered a shallow well. The water was quite good so we filled the bottles, made more tea and sluiced ourselves down.

The wet kit had been placed in the sun to dry and when, turning it over, I chanced to look in the direction of Sumatra, first at the mountains which were shedding the morning mists, then at the distant shore, trying to discover the beach we had sailed from. Hall and I walked down to the beach where a channel had been cut in the coral. Fifty yards from the high-water mark the coral ended abruptly and in sea parlance was 'steep to'. The whole party came to where we had landed the previous evening and dragged the boat along the beach, launching her in the channel. We could not waste time on breakfast, so gathering our belongings, we stowed them away and prepared to put to sea.

When the boat was purchased the bargain included four odd-looking oars, each consisting of a pole five feet long ending in a circular flat disc of basketwork. Now as the last member of the crew stepped aboard, Hall, Good, Birch and Green pulled away. We were immensely pleased to have learned the secret of overcoming the danger from breakers, namely, to land and leave at low tide.

The offshore breeze enabled us to hoist our sail and away we went at a merry clip. This was the ideal way to escape, just sitting down and steering towards freedom while the wind did the work. Thorlby gave us a lesson in how to sail a boat, explaining that you must never tie the sheet, thereby having the craft under control and ready for any emergency. We had not gone more than a quarter of a mile when our expert let the sheet run through his fingers and with a mighty crack, the sail stood away from the mast like a flag, slapping and rippling in the breeze causing the thwart, through which the mast was stepped, to break in two. Down came the mast into the sea, nearly upsetting the boat, and we frantically gathered in the sail. The oars were immediately put out and the boat turned toward the island, while everyone bailed furiously.

The whole business was very depressing. Everything was wet through and the small stock of cigarettes completely ruined, as was Thorlby's reputation as a sailor. The only redeeming feature was that it had happened so soon after leaving the island. It was lucky that the weakness of the thwart showed itself while the sea was calm, and we were so near to land. A few hours later, we should not only have had to row the extra distance but wait for low tide again before we attempted to land. Fortunately, the breakers had not begun to rise, and we landed without much difficulty.

Hall and I, being the only members of Party 14, naturally felt we had more in common. We talked together and did things together. Therefore, as soon as we landed, we began searching for a piece of timber to make another thwart. Finding a reasonably flat piece of wood under some bushes, we dragged it to the boat, where Birch and Good were setting Rowles on the sand. Thorlby told me the padre had horrible sores on his feet and legs and did not want to get them wet. This was the first time I knew we had a casualty in the party, as he had shown no problems in Padang. When the work was distributed, it was agreed he should go back to the hut and make tea for the workers.

Hall, Green and I took turns in hacking a hole in the new thwart using a jack-knife and an axe, which made our hands sore and broke our fingernails. The thwart completed, we placed it over the old one and lashed them together with rope. Meanwhile, Thorlby, Good and Birch had sewn tapes to the sail to enable a reef to be taken in, which our 'expert' now considered essential, saying the sail had been too large. The work had taken two hours and, feeling extremely satisfied, we made our way along the beach towards the hut. We were disappointed to find no sign of tea, fire or the padre. He was inside fast asleep! When I told the padre in no uncertain terms what I thought, he produced, with a sheepish grin, a bottle of wine which none of us had seen before. Realising that this was not the time to start arguments, we accepted his peace offering. The wine was emptied down six thirsty throats and the bottle filled with water. We then retraced our steps to the boat and launched her with some difficulty, as the tide was beginning to flow, and the breakers were getting bigger every moment.

Again we were on blue water, but this time there was not that feeling of reliance upon each other. It seemed each member of the crew was watching the others to see he did only the same amount of work. In this uncomfortable atmosphere, we sailed north-west on a course which we hoped would bring us to Pulau Nias. As twilight deepened, the sea became very choppy and I took the steering paddle from Thorlby.

The canoe curved up high at each end; two feet at the bow and at the stern were decked over. The steersman sat on the deck-head aft, with an oar-bladed paddle. It was a strenuous job trying to manipulate a boat so big with such a small paddle. With a garden-spade handle on top, the paddle was operated by the right hand, needing a slight twist to sail in a different direction. The left hand held the shaft halfway down, gripping it firmly to stop it being pulled away by the dragging action of the water against the side of the boat. After some time, steering became agony.

Seated in the centre of the boat was the padre, who acted as navigator, while Birch, Green, Hall and Good were up forrard, ready to unship the oars and pull her head to sea when necessary. Thorlby was wedged between the padre and the deck-head on which I sat as steersman.

During the night the sea became so rough we were afraid we were in for a real 'Sumatra' [squall] so to lessen the strain on the improvised thwart, as well as our nerves, we downed sail. The boat bucked so alarmingly that I dared not asked anyone to relieve me on the paddle, as the slightest movement might have resulted in disaster.

The oars were put out and the men did sterling work keeping the boat head-on to the sea. My buttocks ached abominably, not being able to move in the wedge-shaped seat, and when I mentioned this to Thorlby he handed me a blanket, which for a short time felt like a seat in paradise. The strain on my arms was almost beyond endurance, and though I had a large blister between the thumb and finger of my left hand because of the twisting motion of the paddle shaft, I hardly knew it existed.

We were tossed about like a cork, but no one was seasick; perhaps we were all too afraid to be ill. Waves came inboard and some had their first taste of bailing. About 9 pm we had 'supper', a tin of bully with two biscuits. Then came the question of water. We found that, apart from the padre's wine bottle, the only other fresh water in the boat was in Hall's bottle and mine. The others had apparently not considered water would be necessary for a mere 100-mile sea trip or that a water bottle was an essential part of their escape kit. Even a boy scout would have carried water for a journey by sea. Severe rationing immediately became necessary and this was one reason why the party finally split.

Cold and shivering, next morning we saw 'white horses' of tremendous size. First, we were on the crest of a huge wave and then went slipping down and down into a water valley. The morale of the crew was shattered and we mere humans were silent in that vast waste of angry sea.

All through that day we struggled against the storm, which appeared to be increasing in intensity. Tempers became short and the strain was beginning to tell on those who were doing the work. The contents of the three water bottles were guarded most carefully, but exposure to the tropical sun and the hard work of keeping the boat headed to sea, coupled with constant bailing, made us very thirsty.

On the morning of 19 March, we found a sea of glass with hardly a ripple and not a breath of wind. The sun rose like a large golden ball, creating a blinding glare on the mirror-like sea and, searching in haversacks, those who had sunglasses put them on. When a cloud in the distance was recognised as land, the discovery put new life into everyone and the petty squabbles of yesterday were forgotten. Estimating the distance between us and the land as thirty miles, we reckoned the evening meal would be eaten ashore. The men took up the oars again and I resumed work with the steering paddle and away we went to a steady in-out, in-out. As the sun rose higher the cloud faded away and we might have been in the middle of the Indian Ocean instead of a few miles from land. In fact, at one time some talked of turning back, but that was only after back-breaking rowing with those horrible makeshift oars for seven hours with still no sign of land. These members of the crew did not apparently realise that it would still be necessary to row back, and it would take no extra work to row forward.

The padre's knowledge of the use of a compass was put in doubt, as every hour or so someone would ask if we were on course and the answer was always the same, 'Dead on'. It seemed astonishing that we had kept such a perfect course and yet could see no land, so I determined to check our navigator's accuracy. I watched the sun, put the boat round by some 60 degrees and asked how we were for course. Immediately came the answer, 'Dead on'. After that we thought it wiser, if we were ever to reach land, to make a change. Thorlby became navigator.

Time sped on but not the boat and, for all the hard work done by the oarsmen, there was still no sign of land. I knew they were tired. The poor chaps were completely exhausted but it was better to have them grouse and curse at my apparent harshness in urging them on than that they should give up when we would probably have drifted back over the miles we had come, ruining our effort to escape. The boat simply crawled along the glassy sea and, to get more speed, the rowers spelled each other while Thorlby and I took turns at steering.

Evening came and visions of supper ashore began to fade. This was our fourth night at sea and the water supply had given out at midday. We were literally gasping for a drink by teatime when Hall produced a small tin of apricots. This was a windfall and although one tin among seven people did not go far, it helped considerably. I remember Green exchanging one of his apricots for the juice in the tin. We all had cracked lips and swollen tongues. Everyone was in bad shape, but still we moved steadily nearer where we knew the island to be. At 11 pm a faint light was seen on the skyline and a bearing taken on it. This literal ray of hope encouraged the oarsmen and on and on they rowed. Midnight came and although the light had long since vanished, we held to the course and soon saw a solid blackness that could only be land. We agreed to attract the attention of the villagers by shouting in unison. We arranged a one-two-three and then shouted as hard as we could. Miracle of miracles, the light appeared again but a little to the south. Shouting again, we struck matches to enable the bearer of the light to see us. Time and again we shouted, '*Kasi tolong*' [give help] and the light moved nearer. Just after 1 am we grounded on the beach 200 yards north of the light and thank heaven there were no breakers. Jumping into the shallows to pull the boat ashore, I stupidly plucked a leaf from a bush, put it in my mouth and began chewing it to try to bring back saliva to my parched throat but the bitter taste made me spit it out.

The light appeared again but this time over to the left and slightly behind us. We thought the men were in a boat and searching for us in the darkness, so we called again and they told us to pull our boat through the shallows towards the light. Grabbing the gunwale, we stumbled over coral and sand, through the shallow water, pushing the boat as fast as we could and soon saw two men holding up a pressure lamp which illuminated the spit of land where they stood. Being the only member of the crew who could speak Malay, I asked for water, whereupon the men suggested coconut milk and if we would follow them they would produce the nuts in a few minutes. Some 150 yards from where the boat lay, we came to a clump of coconut trees and by the light of the lamp watched one of the men climb the nearest long, slender tree and start hacking at a bunch of tender nuts, which soon came tumbling down. It took only seconds for our friends to slice off the tops with their *parangs* [machetes] and we drank deep. Within five minutes everyone had as much to drink as he could desire.

Assuring me the boat was quite safe, our benefactors suggested we take some food, and after a short walk we arrived at a small hut, the door standing wide open. The interior was well lit and we could see three people busy cooking food on an open stove. Inviting us inside, our hosts asked us to be seated on the grass mats on the wooden floor and handed coffee round. Much chatter outside indicated that more villagers were interested in the strangers from the sea. Soon the small house was packed with people, all kindly disposed and willing to help us in every possible way.

When I asked if we had landed on Pulau Nias, our new friends told me that we were well south of it, in fact some 220 miles, and were now on Pulau Sipoera [Sipura]. The reason was our bad navigation and the fact that we had been battling against a strong current which had driven us in a southerly direction.

Soon a magnificent supper of boiled rice and bananas was placed in front of us and with mess tins crammed full to the brim, we ate voraciously while the crowd of villagers jabbered away in a dialect I did not know and which the host, who interpreted, said was Mentawai. The tenant of this house invited Hall, Green and me to stay with him. The other four were taken to a building which had previously been a barracks for Dutch troops. We three arranged our bedding on the floor of the room, the door opening onto the street. Being very tired but happy and excited that we had reached the islands, our next job was to get as much sleep as possible ready for tomorrow. Finishing my cigarette, I looked at my watch. It was already 1.30 am and therefore 21 March.

As dawn broke, we were disturbed by the preparations being made for breakfast and I was amazed that I felt nauseated by the very thought of food. My mouth had a horrible taste which, from past experience, indicated I had contracted fever. Covered with blankets, I stayed in bed and my companions told me Thorlby and the padre had been taken into the village and made contact with an English-speaking native schoolmaster who was in charge of the local hospital. However, he never came to treat me. During the day the fever became much worse and Hall stayed with me while Green went fishing with a native boy. The next two days on that island were a blank, as I had become delirious. When I began to take an interest in living, I found huge suppurating sores had broken out round my neck. These could not have been the result of fever and I could only think it was from chewing the mangrove leaf.

On the fifth morning, I considered I was strong enough to walk. Staggering through the door with the help of my friends, we walked along an earth road to a building fifty yards away, which Hall told me was the communal bathroom. Emerging cleaner but weaker, I was helped back to the hut, where our sympathetic host prepared a cup of strong, black, delicious coffee, which helped me regain my strength. A little later, Birch came to ask how I was and told me the latest news about the 'other' party, making it quite clear that from now on, the four barrack-room boys were one party and we three another. A break was inevitable, but I hardly thought it would show so soon.

Feeling much better for the coffee, I walked unsteadily to the place where we had left the boat. It was the first time I had seen the place in daylight, and I realised why the native men had appeared to be behind us when we landed. A spur ran out into the sea forming a kind of natural harbour. The natives had been standing on the very tip of the land, which we had missed by 200 yards. In the angle which formed the harbour, the sea had eroded the low-lying ground, making a landlocked lagoon at low tide. There, riding at anchor, lay a boat of about five tons' displacement which would have served our purpose excellently. The dugout canoe looked puny beside her but we did not have any money to buy the boat and had not the heart to take it by force after the natives had been so kind to us, but the temptation was almost irresistible.

On my way back to the house, I met the padre and Thorlby. As we debated what to do, neither of them mentioned a split in the party and plans were left indefinite. Over breakfast I discussed the situation with Hall and Green, who both agreed we should get away as soon as possible; whether north or south it did not matter as long as we were moving. While we were weighing up the pros and cons, our host approached and behind him followed another Indonesian. Our benefactor explained this man (indicating the shadow) would pilot us to Pulau Pagai. We jumped at the idea and Green immediately found Thorlby, who also was very pleased that we now had the services of an expert sailor, so we made ready to sail. At 10 am on 25 March, the seven of us embarked again in the canoe with Mat (the Indonesian) in the seat of honour as steersman. Our island friends, who crowded on the jetty, gave us *'Selamat jalan'* and we returned very sincere thanks. Mat hoisted the sail, showing us how a boat should be handled.

Sailing all day with a gentle following wind, we skirted the coast of Sipoera and were rather disappointed when, at about 5 pm, Mat told us that was where he lived and put into a small bay, where we disembarked. Leading us 250 yards along a path fringed with scrub and palms, he reached a native village where he pointed out his home. For sleeping quarters we had a platform of wood slats, not particularly comfortable but very acceptable. The sores round my neck had become very painful and were most repulsive to look at but I managed to keep them covered up; it was essential to protect them at night from mosquitoes. Conversation now centred round the fact that Fate in the shape of Mat had apparently taken a hand in the escape game and as we were travelling south, we decided we must try to get to Australia.

Next morning, with Mat still in charge, we sailed away early. We soon left the land behind and headed for an island in the distance. The wind again was just right, so there was none of that backbreaking rowing. It turned us green with envy to see how easily Mat manipulated the steering, leaving us to admire both his ability and the scenery of the islands. Taking the school atlas from my haversack, I found that Pagai consisted of two islands, Pagai North and Pagai South, with a large lagoon of deep water separating them. Facing the lagoon at the southern end of the northern island was Sikakap, a small village and apparently the most important place in the Mentawai group. This was one of the places the Salvation Army padre had mentioned in Padang. The atlas confirmed the village boasted a *deman* [native magistrate] and was on the route of KPM's (a Dutch shipping company) coastal vessels. The Mentawais were Christians and we could expect help, which made the Europeans in the boat very keen to see this 'Southampton' of the islands.

About 2 pm Mat steered to the right of a sandy reef over which the sea was breaking and, making a ninety-degree turn, we sailed round a small headland and were amazed to see a village. Had we been trying to find the place ourselves I am certain we should have sailed past the entrance. The reef alone would prevent large coastal ships coming in, so it was obvious they must enter through the channel on the Indian Ocean side. The boat was brought expertly alongside a wooden jetty onto which we scrambled, and no sooner had the landing been made than a European came striding towards us. The padre and Thorlby talked to him while the rest of us removed our few belongings from the boat.

I heard the stranger introduce himself as Bakar, chief officer of some KPM ship, but being busy attending to the kit, I did not pay attention. When we had finished, I was surprised to find the three had disappeared and, thinking they were fixing up accommodation, we sat on the jetty awaiting their return. As time passed, I became uneasy and did a bit of scouting on my own. Seeing a police station, I went to it and received a warm reception from the clerk. Understanding our circumstances and our hunger, he immediately organised a meal. Returning to the jetty I told the others a meal would be ready soon and we carried our kit to the Mentawai hospice. There were facilities for a bath, after which we had an excellent meal of fried rice and bananas, rounded off with coffee. At the end of the feast, I discovered that our local friend was the magistrate's clerk. He suggested taking us about a mile to some barracks alongside the lagoon.

Shouldering the kit once more, we set off with our guide along the lagoon road, and nearing the new billet were utterly amazed to see, swinging at anchor, a vessel of some 2,500 tons. Jumping rapidly to conclusions, I thought, as must the others, that our puny efforts to escape had at last been rewarded. I was spellbound, but not blind. I turned to the native and asked him when she had arrived. Listening to the clerk's long harangue, the men gathered round, waiting anxiously to hear my interpretation, which I curtly gave: She's been here weeks, she's full of oil, got a diesel engine, there is no one aboard her and she has no crew. The smiles were replaced by looks of incredulity. We'd been looking for a ship. Here was the grandest chance we had ever had, and yet we could not sail her for she was much too big and our knowledge insufficient. The sweetness turned to anger and gall. Anyhow, there was tomorrow, and we could inspect the ship for lifeboats, which we could sail, and other necessary gear.

We arrived at the barracks and found our room was one in a block of the few completed buildings in an extensive scheme which had been abandoned. We made ourselves comfortable while Mat was transferred from his position as captain of the boat to the honourable and useful one of cook. A further surprise was in store for us when we found twenty-six Indonesian sailors billeted in other rooms of the building. It was from them we learned the story of the sinking of their ship (of which Bakar was the chief officer) by Japanese shellfire, after they had been ordered into the lifeboats, and of the fifteen days' battle against the wind to cover the 250 miles to the island. Asking about the lifeboats, I was told they were moored to a jetty a few hundred yards away, and made a mental note to inspect the boats. I thanked the informant and returned to our section of the building. The thought of that big vessel hung heavily upon us as we distributed our kit in the clean and spacious rooms allotted to our small party. Hall and I occupied one room while Green, Birch and Good occupied the other.

I suggested it might be possible to get Bakar and his sailors to man the diesel ship and, as we were to board her the following day, we should bring our canoe from the landing place to the jetty where the lifeboats were tied up. Hall and Green supplied the energy to bring the boat to her new moorings. Upon their return at 6 pm they described the two beautifully equipped lifeboats which they had minutely examined. They were describing the kerosene stove fitted to each boat when a further surprise on this island of surprises occurred. An unknown European introduced himself as Mr Inglis and told us that my brother officers were living in Bakar's bungalow along with himself and five Belgians, three women and two men.

I was taken aback when he asked why I could not be friends with Rowles and Thorlby. It was necessary to explain that I was aware of the strained atmosphere, but it had been caused by their own actions. I remarked that I had not known where they were until he told me. Vaguely suggesting that I 'square things up' he began to tell us how he came to be on Pulau Pagai, but being naked from the midriff up, and the mosquitoes being active, I excused myself while I put on my shirt as protection. Mr Inglis seemed surprised when he noticed the three 'pips' on my shoulder straps and said, 'That's funny, neither Thorlby or Rowles ever mentioned there was another officer in the party.' We all smiled at this remark and he visibly thawed and became friendly. He told us the story of how he had been a tea planter in Java and had evaded capture by the Japanese by boarding Bakar's ship, finally returning to Pulau Pagai in one of the lifeboats. Mr Inglis left, promising to give us any help within his power.

Getting up early on 27 March, I began the daily task of treating my sores when Green rushed into the room with news that Thorlby and the padre were taking the canoe to give the big ship the 'once over', so Hall hurried out and joined them as our representative. More than an hour passed before they returned and Hall reported not only what he had seen, but also what he had been told. With Bakar's blessing and influence bestowed upon Thorlby and Co., it was a great inducement for all the party to throw in their lot with them, abandoning me to make whatever solo effort I cared to. It might be that they had come to an arrangement with Bakar and his sailors to try to run the Japanese gauntlet across the Indian Ocean or that they were to be given one of the lifeboats with a kerosene stove. As tempting as the proposition seemed, these things weighed not at all with Hall and Green, who remained steadfast in their willingness to accompany me, and as our erstwhile companions never came near the barracks, Private Good gave the message that we had decided to go our own way. So Rowles, Thorlby, Birch and Good would be in one party, and Hall, Green and myself in the other. While on our way to the police station to inquire about prospective boats, we once more met Mr Inglis who, true to his promise to help us, accompanied us in the role of interpreter in Dutch.

Mr Inglis and the magistrate's clerk were most helpful. In scouring the beach we had come upon a small clinker-built dinghy named *Gilca*. She had the usual three seats and a small tiller cockpit. She was seventeen feet long and four feet six inches in the beam.

Getting the deed for transferring the ownership of this boat proved to be a slow business and was left entirely to our two friends. It was finally accomplished by the British government over my signature, promising to pay the Dutch government 250 guilders, this price to include repairs, alterations, food and clothing.

We arranged for new planks to be put on the sides of *Gilca* where there was any doubt. The local boat-building yard, comprising half a dozen men with antiquated tools, undertook the work, and for the quality of the work done I have nothing but the highest praise. Our requirements consisted of a mast, outriggers, a keel, a strengthened rudder and a wooden frame to support a canvas covering.

Seeing the work underway, we returned to our barracks for *tiffin* [lunch]. I was beginning to feel much more my old self. The sores still troubled me but action and preparing the boat for sea so occupied my mind that I had practically forgotten them. After lunch, we decided our party would visit the big vessel to strip her of everything we considered necessary for the journey. So at 2.30 pm, Hall, Green and I sailed the dugout canoe across the lagoon, mooring her under the stern. Her name was (as nearly as I can remember) *Mueewe*. Hall and Green collected paint and ropes (both wire and hemp) and from the engine room returned with valuable loot in the shape of a hammer, brace and drills, while I went forward to inspect the chart room on the bridge, taking charts and a pair of dividers. My friends appeared from the cabins and dumped two mattresses on the deck, saying with a big grin that they were just to make things easier for us.

The next two hours were spent in taking canvas-dodgers [protection from the weather] from the rails and generally interfering with the ship's innards. By this time, the sun was beginning to sink behind the hills and the bells of the Mentawais' little church sounded clearly across the lagoon. Several locals were sculling round the ship in their small craft with the obvious intention of boarding her after we had gone. Lowering the loot into our overladen craft, we returned to shore and, after making several journeys from the jetty to the billet, finally transferred our ill-gotten but useful gains.

Bakar came to our billet with an automatic and naïvely asked Hall to clean it for him as the outside was a little rusty. Hall just as naïvely agreed and retired into the room behind the one in which we were talking, saying he was going to get some oil, cloth and a cleaning rod. In the meantime, Bakar gave us an out-of-date wind chart, telling us that the way to Australia lay wide open, inasmuch as the wind and current were at that time of year set right for the North-West Cape.

With an apologetic smile for having been so long, Hall returned the now beautifully shining weapon to its owner, who loaded it and slipped it into his pocket with a final tap of approbation, accompanied by a sweeping glance which said, 'You see what I mean if you try to take my lifeboat.' We saw and we knew. We knew the weapon was no longer lethal, as Artificer Jackson Hall had filed the striker pin, but the unsuspecting Dutchman put a guard on the lifeboat just in case.

As Hall and I clambered into our beds we had a jolly good laugh. Besides the native police with their old-type rifles, only Hall, Thorlby and I were armed.

The following morning, we continued fitting out *Gilca*. For a water tank, we drained one of the diesel oil drums and placed it on stones. We poured in water, made a huge fire beneath and after four applications of boiling, we voted the drum clean enough for fresh water. We laid it flat, screwed in the iron bung and made a four-inch hole in the top, to which we fitted a wooden plug. The boat seemed to need a keel to help balance the sail and prevent drift, so a twelve-inch by four-inch plank was secured edgeways to the keelson [centre structure] of *Gilca* with six-inch nails, which were clenched inside the boat with caulking on top. We assisted the workmen with construction of the outriggers which were eight feet long and pointed on the leading edge. These riggers were attached to two slightly bent runners with rattan lashings, then firmly lashed at the gunwales. Pegs driven in each side of the runners prevented any lateral movement, while vertical play was minimised by long rattan lashings passing under the thwarts. We were gaining confidence in our little craft and, examining the stout construction of the wooden frame over which we intended fitting the stolen canvas, we began to feel we were making an awful lot of fuss about a bit of a trip to Australia.

The next business was to see about food. Arrangements were made for a seven-gallon drum of rice, two four-gallon tins of banana crisps, fifty coconuts and a dissected cooked goat, the last to be packed in an old petrol tin lined with paper. All this made a sizable pile, not easy to stow.

The Mentawais were particularly kind to us and brought fruit, eggs and chickens. One Indonesian policemen acted as interpreter and through him we were invited to attend their church whenever we desired. As far as I could gather, they were Presbyterians and were exceedingly proud of being Christians. The Mentawai women looked most picturesque in banana-leaf coats and large conical hats, with a sarong for a skirt to complete the ensemble. The men were the most effeminate-looking males I have ever seen. They had no hair on their faces and their skin was as smooth as the women's. Their huge round eyes with long curling lashes, plus a curiously shy manner made them seem almost childlike. Nevertheless, their actions belied their looks. To see them as we did a little time later in stormy weather, handling their frail craft in huge seas, showed their courage was certainly not wanting.

We had to turn to the Indonesians for clothes. We each got a *baju* [jacket] and *sarong* from the local tailor, who had also been engaged to make

*Gilca*'s sail from the stolen canvas. The spare material was to cover the superstructure of the wooden frame built on the boat.

The two workmen carrying out the recommissioning suggested we paint *Gilca*'s bottom and this appealed to my companions, who asked where they could get paint. They pointed us to the boatyard and there we saw Thorlby's craft standing on the slips in all her newfound glory. She had been painted white with a crimson band a foot wide on the waterline. She looked like a bride about to go to her wedding and the bridegroom was fussing around her. Rummaging through the small stock of paint, we emerged triumphant with an 8lb tin of battleship grey. As *Gilca* was painted white with a green top rail, we hoped the grey would provide camouflage proof against Japanese air or surface craft. With three energetic workers slapping on paint, *Gilca* was soon transformed and we had a quiet little ceremony of three really good cups of coffee at the launching. Only the fixing of the water tank remained and this we did by lashing it to the framework of the boat with stay wires taken from lampposts near the police station. For the sail, we took rope from the flagpole in front of the same building.

During *tiffin*, Birch told us Thorlby intended sailing the next day, 1 April, with Mr Inglis as a member of the crew. The date made us all smile, but the information spurred us on with the final job of filling the water tank.

## Chapter 4

# April Fools' Day

1 April, All Fools' Day, saw us up an hour before dawn. A flickering rose-coloured glow through the open window showed that Mat was cooking pieces of goat and beside him was the petrol tin where, wrapped in paper, each piece was to be a titbit to supplement the hard tack.

It was amazing how much carrying we had to do and every pound of weight put into *Gilca* caused a deeper frown on my forehead. The axe, the two-pound hammer, the brace and drills, were they necessary? All these things meant less freeboard and more bailing should we strike rough seas. After countless journeys from the barracks to the jetty, we reached the stage when everything was on board but each of us was certain we had forgotten something vitally important.

After a trial trip round the lagoon to find out how our boat answered the helm, we were surprised to find it was nearly midday. Great activity was noticed in the vicinity of Thorlby's boat, so we ambled down the road and along the jetty.

Then came the problem of what was to be done with the dugout canoe. It was no further use to us and I suggested it be given to Mat as payment for having brought us to Sikakap. At noon precisely, after wishing them Godspeed, we returned to the billet with zero hour fixed for 3 pm.

The minute hand of my watch was pointing to zero. Hall and Green went on board, and our well-wishers, after shaking hands with us, presented me with twenty-five guilders to assist our little expedition in its attempt to escape. It was gratefully accepted. At 3 pm we untied *Gilca* from her moorings and hoisted sail. A few yards from the jetty our friends shouted, 'Bon voyage' and a warning: 'You want more freeboard than that, Captain.' We all knew that and we wanted a larger boat but could do nothing about it. I simply smiled, waved a hand and settled down to steer towards the reef which marked the opening from the lagoon. A course was laid to the southern shore and we tacked steadily towards the entrance. Whether I had the ability to use the wind properly I do not know, but getting away from the reef proved a tricky business. I was pleased when we finally managed it and we could settle ourselves comfortably for a run of 220 miles to Enggano, the most southerly island of the Mentawai group.

*Gilca* sailed beautifully. We talked and sang and wondered if we could overtake Thorlby's boat or Bakar's, which were both on the horizon. Details were worked out regarding duties such as cooking and steering. At this stage, owing to our having so much cooked goat on board, the chef had merely to open a tin lid, and Green volunteered for this job. It was agreed that two meals a day plus a banana or two would be ample. At dusk Green prepared the first meal at sea of goat and bananas, which we washed down with water. We were really too happy and excited to want anything to eat. In fact, we all remained on watch all night as a lovely offshore breeze filled the sail, making it one of the best night's sailing we ever did. On blue water and headed for freedom, we began to feel we were graduating 'in sail' and becoming real mariners.

When morning dawned, we checked our position against the *Mueewe*'s charts. Tracking the coastline with a finger which stopped here and there in doubt, three pairs of eyes scanned the mile of water between *Gilca* and the land. We were utterly amazed to find ourselves near the southern end of Pulau Pagai South. The distance run from leaving Sikakap was, therefore, approximately seventy miles. We were very proud of the achievement with such a heavily laden boat. Australia was 'in the bag' and our morale was twice as high as the mast.

Rounding Sanding like a racing craft, we sailed into the Indian Ocean, and putting the helm over, went south again. Seventy miles away lay a small atoll called Mega and I wanted to make a landfall. This, I thought, would prove our ability to navigate on dead reckoning. All day the wind raged and still we kept the sail up. It was impossible to make a fire, so we ate more fried goat and bananas. This racing was all right but the boat was shipping too much water and steering was really hard work. The angle at which *Gilca* was leaning would, I am sure, have made many a practised yachtsman pray for us. But we green novices were annoyed only at being wet through and having to bail. The constant tearing through the water like an express train finally began to get on my nerves. The steering was like trying to hold a five-ton lorry from skidding on an icy road. I knew the man on the tiller had to watch and feel the wind, otherwise something would be bound to happen. Neither Hall, Green nor I had done any sailing previously, and as Green was the type of chap who would have a smack at most things once, we soon found that once was generally sufficient. Even when painting *Gilca*, he had kicked the paint can over. Remembering this propensity, I felt it in my bones that he could make *Gilca* gibe as easy as pie, so it was Hall who relieved me on the tiller.

Several successive heavy seas breaking inboard convinced us the weather was becoming worse and something had better be done about getting the sail down. This was not easy, and trying to lower it, we found the canvas was being blown away. Green and I struggled with the sail, afraid every minute that the boat would turn over, but our luck held and inch-by-inch the wild flapping piece of canvas was hauled in and made secure. Night had fallen but we had no time to notice anything but the raging sea which came pouring into *Gilca*. We had to lighten the boat as the starboard gunwale was constantly under water, compelling us to bail continuously. We did not realise at the time that the canvas superstructure was partly responsible for this state of affairs. It was decided to jettison the least important items in our larder, namely the fifty coconuts. At about two pounds each, we should gain several inches of freeboard. Speed records were broken in getting the nuts over the side and when the last one was thrown into the sea I checked the additional amount of freeboard gained, but for all the difference I could see, the nuts might just as well have stayed in the boat. The mattresses probably weighed as much as the nuts. We discussed getting rid of them, but as they were the only luxury we possessed it was decided to keep them. Being filled with kapok, they might become useful as life rafts.

As the storm was not abating, Hall suggested putting out a sea anchor. We had never done this before but the term 'riding out the storm' appealed to us and lashing the seven-gallon drum of rice to a five-inch hawser seventy-five feet long, Hall heaved the drum into the sea. We fondly imagined the drum would sink and keep the boat anchored head to sea, but to our consternation the drum floated! It was impossible not to laugh at our utter stupidity and we quickly drew the drum back into the boat before it could damage the planking. We paid out the free end of the rope over the bows, fastening the inner end to the mast, and so we rode out the storm.

We were wet and cold. There could be no thought of sleep for us and the sores on my neck were burning with the saltwater. With a dipper made from bamboo, I got a mug of fresh water from the tank, soaked the sleeve of my *baju* in it and dabbed the sores gently to ease the stinging pain.

A washed-out dawn found the storm abating and we hauled in the sea-anchor rope and made sail once more, wondering how much we had been blown off course. As soon as the sun got stronger, the matches, mattresses and blankets were put on top of the canvas awning to dry. We all voted for a hot breakfast and Green again volunteered to give us our first cooked meal of rice on *Gilca*. This was made possible through a petrol lighter we had bought at Sikakap. The cook soon had a fire going, and with professional nonchalance spied into the can of boiling rice, occasionally smiling at us while he treated us to samples of crooning. When the final, heart-throbbing notes of 'Where the Blue of the Night' faded away, Green found sufficient breath to tell us the feast was ready. The rice was hot, in fact boiling hot, but that was all. Cooked it was not. But rather than wait any longer, we ate it. We pulled Green's leg unmercifully about his cooking ability and I went so far as to say the rice merely wanted two more verses and a chorus and it would have been cooked! He was hurt by our remarks but excused himself because he was not used to the stove. Then he took a nap on the hard boards.

I turned the mattresses over as they were drying quickly. The weather was now beautiful with the boat making good speed. It was miserable not having anything to do, so I suggested taking over the tiller from Hall. He agreed, and waiting until I had the tiller handle, clambered forward past the water tank on the side opposite the sleeping Green. Hall searched about, found the empty tin which had once contained the cooked goat, and busied himself making an oven because the previous unprotected fire, besides being difficult to start, consumed wood at an enormous rate. After much thought, the solution to the problem was apparently overcome, and with two or three imaginary sketches with his finger, Hall put the petrol tin on the thwart ready to be transformed. Grasping the axe, he gave the tin a mighty swipe. The sudden change from dead silence to this terrific din shot the sleeping Green off his boards looking as if all was lost. He rather politely asked Hall if there was not a quieter way of making an oven, and with a 'Can you think of one?' our 'tiffy' resumed operations. We knew no other way, so the appalling noise went on. All bad things come to an end however, and finally he set up his new contraption ready for its trial run at our evening meal.

Laying the fire, the new cook searched in the haversack for the petrol lighter and produced many things, including a jack-knife, before taking out the lighter. I looked at the tin-opener on the knife and could have suggested a much quieter way of making an oven but thought it best not to interrupt the chef. Hall's cooking effort was an unqualified success and Green grudgingly admitted it too. Had there been enough light, we should probably have seen our cook preening himself, but just as we finished our meal of boiled rice, a pungent smell of burning wood filled the boat. Looking towards the now-dying fire in the stove, we were amazed to see flames *behind* it. The foredeck was on fire, but fortunately there was plenty of water around us and the blaze was soon put out. More leg-pulling ensued and feeling full and having had a chance to get his own back, Green took the tiller while Hall and I lay down to sleep on the now half-dry mattresses.

Three days out from Pulau Sanding and with nothing but blue sea around us came the first discordant note. My watch was from 6 to 8 am and waking about 5.30 I found Hall fast asleep at the tiller and off course. So I woke him, telling him to go and lie down. I hoped he had just dozed off and that half an hour would not put us off course unduly. When he woke, I pointed out the danger of going to sleep when we could only rely on dead reckoning. He understood and took my lecture to heart.

Green then started to twit Hall for having gone to sleep and I learned Hall had previously found Green asleep on duty at the tiller and some sixty degrees off course, though he had never mentioned that to me! This made me very angry and I told them off, explaining we were now completely lost. All I knew was Africa was somewhere to the west and Sumatra to the east, just because they could not stay awake for two hours at a time.

The only sensible thing to do was to try to retrace our course, so I put the boat about and sailed her on a course north and east in the hope we might strike Pulau Pagai again.

We were three very dejected sailors on the return trip. All the 'Hello, old boy' spirit had gone, and we hardly spoke. My harangue had a salutary effect and there was no more having forty winks while on watch. Three days later we sighted land and about 9 pm entered a large lagoon. We dropped anchor over the bow to await daylight, hoping then to recognise where we were. It was quite conceivable we were off the coast of Sumatra and morning would bring hordes of Japs on board. Never did I want to see land less.

The entrance to the anchorage was very narrow. On our port bow was a series of small islands connected by a long arm of land fifteen feet above sea level, while on our starboard beam was a forest-covered promontory some 700 feet high, with a white base which next day proved to be a lovely sandy beach extending in a semicircle. No sooner had the rope gone over the bow than preparations were made for the evening meal.

Supper disposed of and watches arranged, the off-duty men composed themselves for sleep, but as time wore on, a roaring noise gradually increased in intensity and eventually became so fantastic the very thought of sleep was impossible. What had been a quiet lagoon when we entered became a crashing, roaring, demented inferno of breakers and we were afraid the boat might drift and be smashed to matchwood. We listened, stared and waited, ready for instant action if it was necessary. In the danger, all our differences were sunk and once again the party became a team. It was a ghastly night and we were thankful to see daylight. At low tide, the breakers we had seen during the night disappeared, leaving only an oily, ugly swirl on the surface of the sea. It was most disconcerting to look over the side of the boat and see through the translucent water the jagged rocky bottom. You could not possibly judge its depth by just looking at it.

We voted to get out of this death trap while the sea was calm. We ran up the sail and hauled in the rope (for which we now had a deep affection). To turn *Gilca* round and put her back on the course by which we had entered this horrible place meant we had to sail over what appeared to be a step. Great pointed green and brown rocks could be seen so clearly on the ocean bed that Hall tried to check the depth with one of the basket oars we had taken from the old dugout canoe. He touched bottom. It was a moot point whether the keel would clear it. This called for action and, in true sailor fashion, the helm was put hard over and *Gilca* showed what sort of a craft she was by immediately responding. Although the rock was under our stern, we cleared the hazard successfully. Three soldier-sailors sailed out through the gates of hell with their blood pressure returning to normal as the distance between *Gilca* and the land increased. About a mile from shore, with the help of the chart, we recognised our previous night's anchorage as part of Sanding Reef, and while Hall made a thanksgiving breakfast, I put our little craft on course for Mega and Enggano. This was 8 April. Our sailing date of 1 April had certainly made fools of us. We wondered how the other party were faring.

During the beautifully serene days that followed, we told stories of our private lives. From these we learned that Green had been a crooner and for hours the quiet of the Indian Ocean was disturbed by *Gilca*'s own private Bing Crosby as evidence of his story. The only other moan on the boat was from me, as my sores were not getting any better, though physically I was feeling very fit, having completely thrown off the fever. Hall related anecdotes of things that had happened to him on his long-distance lorry journeys between Yorkshire and London. We learned of 'Sam's' roadhouse for drivers, the price of the wholesome fare provided and the general goodwill which prevailed in that establishment.

After we were inundated during one storm, we found our matches ruined and the lighter fluid had evaporated which led to another fly in the ointment, a diet of uncooked rice. We had many conferences about this great handicap. The problem was eventually settled more or less by accident.

Talk had centred on everything being as dry as tinder, and in pulling one of the mattresses airing on the awning, the cover was accidentally torn, revealing the kapok. Hall grabbed a handful, suggesting we try the black-powder idea. He cut a piece of wood into very fine slithers, while Green and I exercised the patience of Job in taking the gunpowder from two .38 cartridges, leaving us both with very sore thumbs. One of the blanks was then placed in the revolver, and with the muzzle deep in the kapok, Hall fired the revolver and quickly blew at the spark. The kapok burst into flames, igniting the small sticks. More substantial fuel was gently laid on and soon we had a fire and, what was more to the point, a splendid meal of really well-cooked rice. As we could not keep the fire burning indefinitely, it was decided to cook sufficient rice for four meals or two days. It would have been a waste of food to have cooked any more, as we knew it would not keep longer. Our foresight was justified because that night we encountered bad weather which lasted for four days. The miseries we endured were similar to what had gone before and the sores between our legs, which had a chance to heal while drifting in the doldrums, broke out again.

The sea went down at last and when we woke the following morning, 21 April, we were surprised to find ourselves sailing merrily along near the weather side of Enggano. The coastline appeared to be about 200 feet high and looked black and forbidding, the base being a smother of white foam. We had, therefore, travelled some 200 miles in thirteen days, which was not very good, particularly after our first day's sailing from Sikakap, when we had talked about doing at least 100 miles a day.

The chart showed this island had five small towns or settlements, four of them on the leeside and one on the south coast. As the boat was making such good speed and we were already a few miles past the end of the island we voted to make for the most southerly township. Just after noon and with considerable excitement because this landing was to be the last before Australia, *Gilca* rounded the southernmost spur of the island. Sailing close in, we kept our weather-eye open for the settlement and half an hour later were disappointed to realise the place had been abandoned. A short distance ahead lay a small atoll 450 yards in diameter. As we were wondering how to enter the strait between Enggano and this atoll, which was marked on the chart as Pulau Dua [Island Two], a small boat put out with three natives, who came alongside and told us to follow their boat to the anchorage. Each seemed anxious to outdo his companions in courtesy and assistance. We were guided past a very nasty-looking reef and again the rocks on the seabed were visible. We appeared to be heading for a patch of sandy beach on

Enggano itself, when suddenly our pilot veered 90 degrees west and, round a small headland, we saw several native houses and a small wooden jetty, to which a few minutes later we tied up. There was a small crowd to greet us and they were most generous in giving us coffee and cigarettes.

After the general greetings subsided, I asked whether they had seen any other British soldiers. The headman gave us news of Thorlby's party, saying that they had stayed at Melaconi on the island of Enggano, a dozen miles away, but that five days before they had sailed for Australia. We were amazed at the excellent time they had made from Pulau Pagai. This information fired our ambition to get *Gilca* recommissioned as quickly as possible for her 1,590-mile trip but before we could leave the headman's house the heavens opened and Pulau Dua was deluged with rain. We consoled ourselves that another hour or two would make no difference now, seeing we were so far behind Thorlby's boat. Our friends gave us the latest news about the Japanese advance. Sumatra had fallen and the Japanese flag was flying over all the islands, even on Enggano itself, but so far no Japs had landed, and this island was under the control of Jap-Indonesian agents.

Pulau Dua was, or had been, a port where the KPM ships called for copra. They told us interesting stories about how the present population came to be there. It appeared that none of the people loved their island home. For minor civil offences such as not paying taxes, the Dutch government banished them from Sumatra to Enggano for terms as long as ten years. As I interpreted for my friends, they agreed it was one way of colonising a place. It transpired these twenty-odd people were compelled to live on the southern tip of Enggano, 400 yards across the strait that divided Pulau Dua from the island, and they had to till a certain area of land. Trying to wrest a living from it was a fulltime job owing to the many wild pigs. They also had to prepare shipments of copra for the government on Pulau Dua; this was apparently for the pleasure of living. These people did not like the Dutch or their methods and seemed to enjoy telling us so.

We were relieved when the rain stopped, and the chief suggested taking us to the Rest House. He detailed two of the younger members to act as cook and boy respectively and in a small procession we wended our way to the most imposing building on the atoll, along the only street, a small muddy road. We passed about twenty small huts and under the verandah of one I noticed a map showing the shipping routes round the Netherland East Indies, which I earmarked for possession. Once at the Rest House, our informant told us the place was used by the Controlleur upon his rare visits to the place. The building consisted of a lounge, three bedrooms, one of which was being used as a store, a kitchen and a mod. san. lavatory. An adjacent well appeared to be the only bathroom. I asked the cook to provide a meal, and while this was being done we enjoyed a bath and a general brush-up. After an excellent meal, we returned to *Gilca* and took everything out of her for a spring clean. Several journeys to the Rest House were necessary before we had all our belongings stored away, we hoped, from prying eyes. The mattresses were torn open and the kapok scattered about in the sun to dry. The water tank was drained and oiled externally.

Our next task was the washing down of the boat itself, as it had become really filthy with ashes from the fire. Tins of water were being poured into *Gilca* when one of the villagers cried out, '*Laya!*' [Sail ho!] and, pausing in our work to look where he was pointing, we saw coming from the south a boat which we recognised by her rig and colour as Thorlby's. All work stopped, and Hall, with one man, put off in a small canoe to meet the red-and-white painted craft. When they were only about a quarter of a mile apart, it veered east and, running before a good breeze, the vessel soon rounded Enggano Point, leaving Hall and his companion to paddle back to Pulau Dua. Seeing Thorlby's boat spurred me on and I badgered Green to get *Gilca* bailed dry so we could re-lash the water tank in its old position. He worked slowly and silently; I could tell something was brewing. Hall returned and I asked if he could see any damage to Thorlby's boat. When he said no, we wondered why it had returned. Perhaps it was for repairs and if so, we should be able to sail in convoy. This, we thought, would make the long journey much pleasanter.

Time was precious and we were anxious to be ready in case Thorlby's repairs were only minor. Arrangements were made with the headman to find us a carpenter. We were disappointed to find it would be necessary to send a runner to Melaconi, but there was nothing to be done, so we agreed, impressing on the messenger the importance and urgency of his mission. I was happy to hear Melaconi had a market as this meant the time of waiting would not be wasted. We could purchase many useful things such as matches and perhaps petrol. A list of requirements was made and repeated to the runner until he was word perfect when he recited it, then we saw him into the canoe which would take him across to Enggano. We could do nothing more that day, so returned to the Rest House to try to possess our souls in patience.

Our quarters were brightly lit by wicks floating in a huge shell filled with coconut oil. The table was laden with steaming rice and fruit, which we soon devoured. A homely atmosphere filled the Rest House in strong contrast to our wet and miserable nights in the boat. Through the open door we could see the treacherous, placid ocean lapping on the sand ten yards from where we sat. It certainly felt grand to put one's feet on firm ground and be done with that everlasting rocking. Hall chattered enthusiastically about the work to be done the next day, but Green could not be induced to pass an opinion and left us saying he was going for a walk.

Dismissing Green from our thoughts, our talk turned to food and we both agreed the rice our present cook was giving us was far better cooked than anything we had ever done. We therefore decided to hang around the kitchen at mealtimes to learn the technique of boiling rice. After chatting about the boat and Thorlby's return, we had just agreed to turn in when the low, throbbing beat of a tom-tom sounded. Wondering if it was a signal, I stepped out into the moonlight and a long, low wail caught my ear. Calling Hall, I asked him to listen. Turning his head towards the sound, a big smile creased his face and with a 'Come on, Skip' we walked towards the jetty. Wading through the scattered kapok which looked like snow, we came upon a small bunch of people, one of whom was rhythmically beating time with his hand on the end of a six-gallon empty oil drum accompanying Green, who was soulfully rendering 'Moonlight and Shadows' from the film *The Jungle Princess*. The orchestra was our cook and the admiring audience the population of Pulau Dua.

The following morning, we woke early and found cups of tea waiting for us with a tin of hot water for shaving. Tea over, we spent a painful half hour in beard cutting and shaving, which took ten years off us.

After a breakfast of fried eggs, toast and delicious coffee, we were surprised to see ushered into our quarters a villager who was introduced as the carpenter and wanted to know our requirements. I explained that a higher gunwale was the first essential and we would be pleased if he could fit nine-inch planks round the boat apart from the back transom in the tiller cockpit. We also required a bowsprit three feet long. The native craftsman said he would have the work completed in one day and his optimistic view buoyed us considerably.

To replenish *Gilca* with fruit we needed to contact the natives on Enggano proper, so at 11 am Hall and I crossed the strait and followed a track for two miles inland, where we came across a village of twelve huts. Each had a garden with a stockade to prevent damage by wild pigs. The natives here were very, very poor and their living conditions were appalling. Nevertheless, we received what little hospitality they could offer in the shape of the largest, sweetest and most delicious bananas I have ever tasted. We arranged for fruit and other kinds of food to be delivered to us on Pulau Dua and returned to help the optimistic carpenter.

During the hour we had been away, our woodworker had certainly got moving. By the side of a few planks lay a roughly fashioned bowsprit; he had disappeared in search of six-inch nails. Green was nowhere to be seen so we waited by the boat until the carpenter returned with the nails and helped him fit the bowsprit. The job was only half completed when a long, low moan made the workman lay down his tools and look across the strait. Following his gaze, we saw a thin column of smoke rising into the still air. He said he would have to leave us. We felt rather annoyed about this and asked the meaning of the moan and the smoke signal. He explained the horn was to tell the population on Pulau Dua to look for the signal which meant someone was coming. Nothing we could do would make him change his mind. He downed tools and returned to Enggano, promising to return the next day and with this we had to be satisfied. We carried on the work of fitting the bowsprit, cursing all smoke signals.

We were worried by the news. Clearly, he would not want the Japanese to find him working for Europeans. Could it be Japanese who were coming? Surely this signal would not be given if it were only native messengers returning from Melaconi. It must be strangers and if they were Japanese, our effort to escape was over and the three of us could (and we presumed would) be eliminated. Our names would be filed in the archives reserved for the missing, presumed dead. We rushed the work on the boat and during the afternoon our fears rose to fever pitch as a boat rounded the point, turned into the strait and made directly for our jetty. We were greatly relieved to find it was Captain Thorlby, Mr Inglis and four natives. As we helped our comrades from the boat to the jetty, there was considerable leg-pulling about the fright they had given us. I mentioned the possibility they were Japanese at which point Thorlby introduced the largest of the natives as Marinas, a Jap-Indonesian agent. On my asking what the deuce he was doing there, Thorlby wearily said it was a long story. Inviting them along to the Rest House, I noticed that Marinas was following and told him to stay where he was. Thorlby asked me not to be angry with him, as he had been decent with them. Green, Hall and I clustered round our visitors to hear their news. Thorlby's story went as follows:

'On 18 April, we set off from Melaconi on a compass bearing of 144 degrees to try to reach North West Cape, Australia, but after the second day out we encountered bad weather with contrary winds. We tacked about and hoped the sea would moderate and for the next three days, although constant bailing was necessary, we kept the boat headed south. Not only did the weather become worse, but to our dismay we found the water in the bilge increasing at such a rate that our fears she was leaking were confirmed. We therefore decided by a majority of votes to turn back and try to make Enggano. On the return trip, the rope jammed in the pulley block during bad weather and we could not lower the sail. I had to be hauled up the mast with a rope. This was a nerve-racking experience with such a heavy sea running.

'We were extremely pleased to see land again and docked at the same place from which we had left. This man, Marinas, is a Japanese-Indonesian agent and we have given ourselves up to him. We have had enough of the sea.'

Mr Inglis corroborated Thorlby's story, adding many more details. These two were firm friends, having lived through awful experiences together, and it was with all sincerity that they asked us to give ourselves up to the agent. They told us we did not have a dog's chance in our small boat. Neither of them would accept Green's place when he offered it to them, as he was unwilling to accompany Hall and me any further. Giving themselves up had been made easy, as Marinas was to house and feed the party for 50 guilders until they were handed over to the Japanese. But Hall and I wanted freedom and were prepared to fight for it. There could be no giving in for us.

I would have agreed with anyone that to set off on a 1,590-mile journey across the Timor Sea in a seventeen-foot dinghy without any sailing experience whatever, except that gained since leaving Singapore, was a hare-brained scheme, but what else could we do? I did not want to be captured and neither did Hall, so we had to try this crazy journey. Even with the awful experience I now possess, I would try it again rather than fall into the hands of the Japanese.

Thorlby and Inglis agreed to stay the night in our Rest House, so we killed the last remaining chicken and gave them and ourselves 'big eats', finishing off with fruit salad sprinkled liberally with the usual desiccated coconut. For wine, we drank coconut water. Over coffee and cigarettes, they told us more of the awful journey they had had and when I again offered either of them a place in our boat, they promptly and flatly refused, reiterating that we hadn't a chance. This made Hall and me smile, as we were apparently taking part in our own funeral feast.

Arranging mattresses on the floor, the five of us turned in, my partner and I with one eye open for Mr Marinas. We kept the oil lamp burning all night. Lying down chatting, our friends fell asleep one by one, to be rudely awakened about 1 am by violent earth tremors. In the light of the lamp we could see our wooden building swaying. The earthquake lasted about five minutes and was most unpleasant. The volcano Krakatoa, 120 miles away in the Sunda Straits, was obviously responsible and it was some time before we got to sleep again.

The following morning, Green and our friends left and wished Hall and me 'Bon voyage'. Green shook hands with us and there were no hard feelings. One humorous incident occurred when we were each given a list of their home addresses for use if we got safely away. This we thought amusing after their blunt assertions that we hadn't a dog's chance. It looked now as though they were not quite so sure. One thing which gladdened our hearts was their promise to send us some tins of sardines by a native runner to help to stock our larder.

As soon as they pulled away from the jetty, Hall and I were hard at work. Now we were alone, we felt we had a reasonable chance of success. We thought of the additional freeboard gained without Green's large body. We were also encouraged by the return of the carpenter who, like all the locals, had been invisible during the visit of Marinas. He now made up for lost time and we hoped the quality of his work would not suffer. The planks to increase the freeboard were fixed with a butt joint; however, Hall did not approve. He suggested we rifle the storeroom in our billet and see whether it contained anything to strengthen them. Avoiding the cook-caretaker, we were soon in the store, feasting our eyes on packets of screws, nails, black-japanned T-hinges and casement stays. We carried these valuable items to our boat and over each butt joint we screwed two hinges, making a much stronger and more satisfactory job. Next, we stole a bed sheet from the store to make what we blithely called a jib sail. We were confident this would add ten miles a day to our estimated and optimistic hundred, besides enabling us to sail closer to the wind, whatever that meant. The food we had ordered began to arrive and so did nine tins of sardines from our friends at Melaconi. The tins were very rusty but we had no doubt the contents were good. They were Japanese sardines in chilli. We scraped the tins and oiled them to prevent further rusting.

The commissioning of *Gilca* was nearing completion. The water tank was securely lashed and the tedious job of filling it from a well was undertaken. None of the locals would help us in this work and we were extremely glad when the final tin, giving us 44 litres of fresh water, was poured in. We went to a secluded area of the beach, laid out the bed sheet and began sewing the ropes to it. Time slipped by and it was after 2 pm before the work on the sail was completed and the only Chinese on the island came and offered us food. Busy with our task we had forgotten lunch and this Malay-speaking Chinese boy reminded us we were hungry. From a small canoe, he produced a freshly caught fish which he suggested I should eat. Seeing the look of revulsion on my face, he took the fish from me and bit a chunk out of its back and again handed it to me. I closed my eyes and sank my teeth into the glistening scales. The flesh of the fish came away easily and, as I chewed, I found the taste was not unpleasant. Hall also tried this novel way of eating fish, while the boy explained this fish was called *ikan merak* [red fish] and to eat it raw was the correct way. I asked this lad to sell us some fishhooks, but he would not, implying they were more valuable than gold on the islands. I did not press the point and Hall and I returned to the important work of preparing *Gilca* for her long voyage.

The cook suggested our staple diet should be *saygan*, as this was the food always taken by the Indonesians on long sea journeys or out fishing. This is a mixture of equal parts of powdered rice and desiccated coconut. A sample of this hard tack was prepared for trial. Eight or nine spoonfuls were put on a plate and a little water poured over the mixture. After waiting a few minutes, the *saygan* swelled up and the cook told us the food was ready. We were both pleasantly surprised to find the mixture very tasty. We named it 'native porridge' and for short, NP.

On our way to Enggano we had kept a careful check on the amount of rice for one person for one day and found that two four-gallon tins of rice would be ample for two persons for sixty days. Therefore, with two additional tins of *saygan*, we were convinced we should not be faced with a food shortage.

An order was placed immediately for two four-gallon tins of NP and three women came over from Enggano, complete with wooden pestle and mortar, and began making the powdered rice. Half a day later, our stores were increased by two tins of *saygan* and with the return of the messenger from Melaconi, plus the completion of our personal order on Enggano, they now included:

> 2 four-gallon tins of rice (uncooked)
> 2 four-gallon tins of *saygan*
> 1 four-gallon tin of fried chicken
> 1 four-gallon tin of banana crisps
> 9 tins of sardines

3 bunches of bananas
5 dozen hard-boiled eggs (we later found half were bad)
6 packets of *gula java* [palm sugar]
5 pints of coconut oil
1lb tea
1lb coffee
50 coconuts
6 boxes of matches
A few mangoes, pineapples and cucumbers

Hall was a non-smoker so for myself I added a pound of tobacco and a thousand straws from which to make cigarettes. The work on the boat was finished. We paid off the carpenter and went to the Rest House for our last evening on Pulau Dua, feeling happy that our preparations were practically complete. After supper, two weary soldiers lay down and were soon asleep.

The cook and early morning tea came with the dawn, and as the sun gained strength I walked to the edge of the sea. Taking the small army compass from my pocket, I took a bearing on Mount Dempo, 12,000 feet high and 120 miles away. Checking the bearing with the chart, I found an error of five degrees would have to be added to the dead reckoning of 145 degrees to North West Cape, and that sailing along this line would take us to Christmas Island.

We packed our stores in the bottom of the boat and again filled the space under our beds with coconuts. We agreed to leave the mattresses behind as we were going to live hard. Many journeys to and from our quarters were necessary before everything was aboard. We gave our few remaining guilders to the boy who had been cooking for us, laughing that Dutch currency would be useless in Australia. Having eaten our midday meal, we thanked the cook and handed him the money. He was very grateful and said he could pilot us past the reef in his canoe.

At 3 pm on 1 May 1942, we made ready to sail. As we rounded the reef, our guide waved and turned about. We shook out the jib and *Gilca* gathered way quickly. We were again on the blue water. Pulau Dua began to fall behind and our brave little craft was breasting the rollers of the Indian Ocean. At last we were on the long leg, Australia bound. Our great chance had arrived, and nothing lay between us and freedom except the ocean. It was only a matter of time before we reached security Down Under.

## Chapter 5

# The Long Leg

Hall, twenty-eight years of age, stood 5ft 9in. He was ginger-haired, well-built and a non-smoker. A Yorkshireman by birth, he was handy, adaptable and capable, but he could not swim. I was forty-two years of age, 5ft 7in in height, a heavy smoker, a poor swimmer and also a Yorkshireman.

We started the voyage by securing everything against the possibility of a storm. Hall was silent and thoughtful, staring back at the fast-receding land. To cheer him I sang light-hearted songs while steering the boat through a veritable meadow of floating grass. Toward the evening of 1 May the breeze freshened and sailing was a great delight. *Gilca* made rapid progress with her new jib sail, and in a glorious sunset the land faded from our view. We had learned at school that a red sky at night was a sailor's delight. It certainly was ours. We forecast fine weather, and lighting our stove, cooked a really good rice meal. The hours we had spent in the cookhouse on Pulau Dua learning from the cook had not been wasted. Watches of three hours on and three off were arranged but as neither of us felt tired we sat and talked far into the night, sailing dead on course.

2 May dawned and the breeze became light and tricky, causing us to tack west then east. Hall became his usual cheerful self now that land had disappeared and we had metaphorically burned our boats. He knew there would be no turning back. Handing over the tiller to him, I pulled out a small wooden box we called the safe which contained the ship's valuables: revolvers, boxes of matches wrapped in oilskin, folded charts, a pair of dividers and a Bible. (The last was the only reading matter we had on board.) With the aid of the dividers and a protractor cut from one of the charts, I prepared a new chart and started a logbook. Estimating our speed at three knots, I plotted the distance for the past nineteen hours. After comparing the very short line with the great blank space which was the ocean yet to be crossed, I quickly folded the chart and put it back in the safe. I turned my attention to the practical problem of cooking breakfast and airing the blankets.

Discussing the merits of sunbathing I suggested we each stand in the sun for ten minutes the first day and increase the time by five minutes daily, as I considered this would keep us fit. Hall was a bit doubtful, as he had that type of freckly skin which turned red and would not brown no matter how long he stood in the sun. Anyway, he said he would give it a trial. We therefore took off our shirts and enjoyed ten minutes of the morning sunlight.

We chattered about many things, but the talk always returned to our immediate wellbeing, the most vital being food. We agreed that two meals a day would be sufficient as we were not using much energy. All day, contrary winds made steering difficult and towards evening the wind rose and seas came inboard, compelling us to start bailing with the coconut shells. Dropping the mainsail, we carried on under the jib. The new sail was really proving its worth.

All through the night the gale blew from the south-east but in the morning, it swung round and gave us a fair run. I entered two knots in the logbook for our second day at sea and pricked the distance off on the chart. Considering we had had a bad night I suggested a leg of chicken each had been richly earned. I opened the lid of the tin and discovered a most awful smell. We realised the meat had gone bad or at least the oil had turned rancid. As we had plenty of other food, we dumped it over the side. We knew the seriousness of this action but were confident we could re-provision at Christmas Island. If the chicken had gone bad, we worried about the *saygan*. The desiccated coconut might ferment, so we agreed to eat the NP before the rice. This meant cold meals, but there would be hot coffee to finish with.

For hours on end we sat and chatted about our families, homes, work, pleasure and the kind of things we should really like to do but our minds always turned back to reaching freedom as quickly as possible. We believed that after we had been posted missing for six months, the War Office would tell our families we were presumed dead. This worried us intensely, as we did not wish to cause them any unnecessary grief when here we were just sculling around the Indian Ocean, more or less enjoying ourselves. We told each other how we would pull the escape off and make the other party feel sick for having given themselves up.

As the days wore on, we became so sick of the porridge that we decided on one NP meal and one rice meal. Another fact which worried us was the constant tacking to make any use of the wind. Day after day the routine of putting the boat about became monotonous, tacking ten miles east and ten miles west to get a miserable six miles south. The chart had so many jagged lines running across the straight line of the course that it was pure desperation which enabled us to remain hopeful that we could reach Australia.

Then came storms such as I had never seen before, certainly not viewed from a small boat. *Gilca* was tossed about like a cork and needed constant bailing. Fear helped us in getting the boat dry and we substituted the chicken tin for the little coconut shells. Using this, it was possible to remove two or three gallons at a time but it was much harder work. We got used to being wet through and lying down in a blanket we had just wrung the water from.

During fine periods, Hall would tell me stories of his life in Civvy Street: how he had worked as a chauffeur for a doctor and as a van driver for a bakery, and of his adventures, amusing and otherwise, in both jobs. So, the kaleidoscope of Hall's life was shown to an audience of one somewhere in the Indian Ocean.

About this time, I was unfortunate enough to lose my clothes. Having fastened them securely to a thin grass rope, I flung them into the sea to wash them, towing them in our wake. For what seemed like hours I kept an eye on them but a particularly spicy story of Hall's distracted me and when I next looked, they had gone and all I had was a frayed rope end. The boat fairly rocked with my friend's laughter as he twitted me about how easily I could sunbathe. It made me smile too and though it was not unpleasant to be free of clothes, I felt unsightly and wondered what I should do when we arrived at a civilised place. The following day Fate gave me my revenge. I had the laugh at Hall's misfortune in losing his shorts in precisely the same way after he had boasted about the knots which he said Houdini himself could not escape from. Apparently we had fish following us that knew a thing or two about short-circuiting knots, as again we merely had the frayed rope end. We began to look worse than I imagine Robinson Crusoe ever looked, particularly when Hall took off his flapping shirt to save it for 'going ashore' in.

Soreness again began to annoy us and large red patches appeared between our legs. The skin peeled off, leaving a wet, painful blotch like tearing the skin off a blister. The only treatment possible was periodic dabbing with a mixture of fresh and saltwater.

About the twentieth day out, while enjoying a spell of reasonably good sailing, we were both surprised to feel something hit the underside of the boat. My first reaction was the keel had come adrift, so while Hall leaned over the starboard side, I leaned over the other trying to get a glimpse of the makeshift keel. Hall said in a hushed voice, 'See that, Skip?'

'See what?' I replied. The words were hardly out of my mouth when several huge shapes glided underneath. Sharks! They were the first we had seen. We wondered which one had our clothes. From the safety of our boat they were interesting to watch.

After a while we lost interest in our new companions. I had just made the fire for another meal when a terrific bump hit the boat, followed by a splintering of wood and an excited steersman calling, 'Skip, Skip!' Turning, I saw Hall hanging over the rear transom and I made records in hurdling over seats to the cockpit. The rudder had been smashed by the sharks and the saddles through which the pintle fitted were torn off. Hall was straining to prevent the whole thing from floating away. Heaving and grunting, we managed to retrieve the steering apparatus and pull it inboard, where we not only repaired it but strengthened the wood leaf. Hall's ingenuity showed itself as he unscrewed the first of our hinges securing the false freeboard and bent it circular to take the pintle. It was naturally very slack, but the improvised saddle allowed us to put *Gilca* back on course. Anyhow, it was now impossible for the rudder to break adrift, or so we thought.

Each day sharks followed the boat and we became interested in their quick, vicious movements, chiefly because there was nothing else we could take an interest in. At close quarters, they looked rather a sporty type of fish. They were certainly not shy and would stay within a couple of yards of our rudder for hours at a time, with small striped pilot fish always just a few feet in front.

While trying to cook our twenty-first evening meal, we suffered a great misfortune. I struck the last match in the box and the wind blew it out. Hall groaned loudly. We had been very careful when lighting matches but our estimate of three matches a day was obviously short, when taking into account the heads that came off and the number that broke. But our chief enemy was the wind. To make tea or coffee was now a slow business entailing a whole night's steeping to produce even an approximate taste. Still, we had plenty of food and water, and although conditions could have been better, we did not grouse. My tobacco and straws were of no use now, so I reluctantly threw them over the side. Strangely enough, although a heavy smoker, I never once craved a smoke during the rest of the voyage.

That morning I had asked Hall to keep a sharp lookout as we should sight Christmas Island any time now, and as evening gathered we discussed the likelihood of sailing past the island in the darkness. The compass was beginning to show signs of wear. Most of its luminosity had disappeared through being constantly deluged with seawater. This made steering difficult during the night. Our hopes were lifted high as five miles away on our starboard bow we sighted what we thought was a submarine. Altering course towards it, our hopes were dashed as we saw two large trees floating, both covered with gulls. At the same time, grass, leaves and seaweed came past *Gilca* in abundance, so we had every reason to think we were near land. According to the course plotted on our chart, that land must be Christmas Island. Every minute of every hour we were on our toes, looking at all points of the compass for land. But although we strained our eyes to pierce the distant haze, we searched in vain. That night a storm broke, so we downed sail and put the sea anchor over the bows, hoping that we would not drift too much and that we might see the island the next day.

Dawn broke to find two very wet and tired men. Several times our tiny vessel was bailed dry and allowed partially to fill with rainwater so that we could fill the water tank, but a wave would come inboard to spoil the whole lot, setting us frantically bailing again.

For seven weary days and nights we lay to the sea anchor. It could only be our water tank keeping us afloat. The tins of food were small moving islands and even the bed boards across the thwarts floated. This meant *Gilca* was full of water to within less than eight inches of the true gunwale. To make things more unpleasant we were cursed with salt sores once again but had no time to worry over such comparative trifles. It seemed we were in a storm centre and the sooner we got away from this place the better. We could not endure the bailing and the constant lack of sleep. In a great last effort, we once more got the boat reasonably dry and lay down, utterly weary, to await the next water invasion.

Although neither of us wanted to miss making a landing on Christmas Island, common sense told us we could not possibly carry on much longer without sleep and after holding a brief conference we agreed to push on towards Australia. We had no idea how far the boat had drifted, and visibility was so poor that hopes of ever sighting the island were practically nil. From an unknown reserve of strength, we pulled the rope inboard and got under way. Our knowledge of navigation was basic, but logic told us we were being pushed west by the south-east monsoon, and the yard-high canvas hood over our sleeping quarters was acting as a sail. We therefore decided to cut down the wood frame by twelve inches, reducing the wind pressure by at least six square feet on the side of the boat. It was first necessary to evolve a system of fastening that would become the free ends of the frame to the odd foot or so of existing woodwork. This difficulty we overcame by taking every alternate screw from the metal angle brackets securing the thwarts to the frame of the boat. Hall then began to hack with the axe on the starboard side and soon had the four supports a foot shorter. While he had the flying ends, I cut through two of the portside supports and then rushed to help him, securing two of his supports with the screws.

We finally accomplished the work on the awning in the ratio of one support to one spell of bailing, but we felt something worthwhile had been achieved. Unfortunately, our logic did not take us far enough. Had we only turned our boat around and followed the wind, we might have made our estimated 100 miles per day and reached the Cocos Islands, Mauritius or Madagascar; in any case, we could not fail to hit Africa. That this would require sailing 3,000 miles in our boat would not have meant a thing to us. We had implicit faith in *Gilca* after the storms she had withstood. There was nothing courageous in this attitude. Hall could not swim at all and I certainly could not swim three miles, therefore if the boat were to sink within sight of land it would not help us. We might as well be 3,000 miles from land as three. Unfortunately, our faith in Chief Officer Bakar remained unshaken. He had said the wind and current would be set right for Australia. During our first fifty days, the wind was favourable for only two. The current we could not check, so day after day, hoping the wind would change, we held to our course.

Twelve hours after we had made the decision not to land on Christmas Island, the sea moderated. It allowed us to fill our water tank and have enough left over for a much-needed freshwater bath. The following morning, precisely eight days from the time we had dropped our sea anchor, the sun shone once more, lifting our spirits considerably. The wind, though still from the south-east, was moderate and constant tacking was necessary, but we enjoyed some good sailing. The conversation at this time centred upon how amazed the people at North-West Cape would be when our little seventeen-foot *Gilca* came creeping up out of the sea, though we hoped to be sighted by patrolling aircraft when we were about 500 miles from Australia and have help sent to us.

As the fortieth morning of our voyage broke, I opened the safe and produced dividers and chart, plotted the previous day's run and announced proudly to Hall that, according to my reckoning, we had just crossed the fourteenth degree of latitude. He asked what that meant in plain English and I explained about degrees and that North-West Cape was on the twenty-second of these mysterious and imaginary lines, so we had eight more to cross, or approximately 500 miles of ocean, to complete our journey. The jubilation of *Gilca*'s crew knew no bounds. At any moment reconnaissance aircraft might come roaring overhead, to say nothing of sighting surface craft while crossing the shipping lanes.

The weather had become much cooler and what remained of the coconut oil had solidified into a white mass like lard. We sat at the tiller with blankets wrapped round our naked bodies and although the temperature caused us some slight discomfort, it was the most obvious indication we were getting away from the tropics. Chattering about which museum we would put *Gilca* in, I prepared breakfast. In celebration of crossing latitude 14 degrees S, I issued an extra spoonful of porridge each, poured on the water, and while waiting for it to swell, we agreed that Perth Museum could have the boat. Handing Hall his plate and spoon, I turned to pick up mine, and before I could start eating, he retched violently and spat the stuff into the bilge. I was amazed and asked what was wrong with him. He told me frankly there was nothing wrong with him, it was the blasted porridge, and I should try it myself. I did and I too was retching and vomiting. The reason was all too clear. The stuff had become impregnated with saltwater; the question was how. Each tin was fitted with a press-in lid, making it watertight. We carefully examined the sides and the bottom and found minute holes with a tell-tale ring of rust round each. The awful fact was that all our food was uneatable.

For a few minutes neither of us spoke. We had to acknowledge defeat and accept the grim fact that we had no food, except two inches of solidified coconut oil in a beer bottle. Poking this out with a stick, we shared it as our breakfast. Hall was certain that one tin of sardines remained so we practically tore the boat apart, but it was not to be found and we now regretted having varied our diet with rice, sardines and coconuts.

I again produced the chart, carefully studied the distance from Australia, and put these two questions to Hall: 'Do you think we can sail south twenty-five miles a day?' And 'Do you also think you can last twenty days without food?' Hall's answers were typical of the man. To the first question his answer was a plain 'Yes!' To the second, without any hesitation, he replied, 'I'll try, Skipper. A chap once came to my hometown and starved for twenty-four days in a glass cage. It was tuppence to go in. If he could do it, I reckon I can starve for twenty!' If we could do it, Australia was in the bag and we could make land under our own sail. And there was always that tantalising hope of being picked up.

Silences grew longer between us, each sitting with his own thoughts staring at the horizon during the day and at the stars of the Southern Cross at night, steering a course which we hoped would bring blessed relief. Our ignorance of astronomy was appalling; neither of us knew that to sail 'on the Cross' would take us nowhere near our objective. I have since been told that to steer by the Southern Cross you must draw a line through its longer axis to the horizon and that point is three degrees off true south. Being blissfully unaware of this, we continued on our course with never a thought of returning to Sumatra and certain capture.

We must have looked a strange pair, both naked. The skin on Hall's body had assumed a tender rose pink due to exposure. A thick, matted thatch of flaming red hair reached nearly to his shoulders, with a shaggy red beard. In contrast to Hall, my skin was burned to the colour of an Indonesian. My hair and beard were just as long, liberally streaked with grey. Being painfully thin, we suffered excruciating agony from the huge sores on our thighs. We would wake from uneasy slumber with a feeling of intense pain from the inside of the knee, caused by the weight of the other knobbly knee which had been resting on it. Much massaging was necessary before we could get any relief.

One morning I woke before the dawn due to the knee trouble and took over from Hall at the tiller. With a curt 'Of course' he scrambled past me to his bed. We had no energy to waste on speech these days and while rubbing my knee with one hand, I guided *Gilca* with the other.

In the early light, I searched the horizon for land but a great heavy tiredness seemed to have descended upon my eyes and for a moment or so I thought I was going blind. Trying to focus on objects in the boat was slightly easier but while staring at the compass I found that, provided I did not try to open my eyes wide, the heaviness did not bother me. An hour or so later a groan warned me that Hall was waking up, and with much stretching and yawning, he finally sat up. He turned towards me, and with his shaggy mane framed against the canvas of the sail, remained stock still, staring. Then his jaw dropped, leaving a gaping hole in the upper half of his beard. His hairy face looked almost inhuman as he looked at me through tiny slits. For several moments, there was complete silence until I asked what had happened to his eyes. The spell was broken and in a cracked voice he asked, 'Have you seen yours, Mick?' Not having a mirror on board, we both looked over the starboard side of the boat into shadowed water. Our reflections were, indeed, most unpleasant. The eyelids and the soft cavities under the eyes had swollen like huge water blisters, making us look like gigantic bullfrogs. It is perhaps an interesting medical problem why we both had this complaint at precisely the same time. We had been starving now for fourteen days and neither of us had had an evacuation since the food had been found to be contaminated. In fact, food did not greatly interest us during our waking hours. We became quite content to sit and drink water, chatting on rare occasions about our families and the time we would have when we got to Australia.

The awful days dragged by and many times during my turn at the tiller I looked at Hall's tousled head as he lay, sometimes talking or shouting in his sleep, and wondered what was to become of us. Would *Gilca* be found with just two skeletons to bear witness to our fate? Or would she sink without trace, earning for us the cryptic: 'Missing, presumed dead?' These morbid thoughts obsessed me. I repeatedly shook them off and found I had been on the point of dropping off to sleep. Although we both had violent and fanciful dreams, neither of us reached the stage of hallucinating about seeing land. Rather, we believed our previous lives had only been a dream and we had always lived in this tiny boat on the sea. There was no such thing as land; it was a myth. To look over the side was dangerous, for the sun made a deep cone of light through which large fantastically coloured fish glided lazily. It appeared to be so cool and wonderful down there, so soft, silent and restful, yet I always thought of loved ones and of my pal lying there asleep. It was necessary at these times to get hold of my mind and metaphorically pull up the old socks, to do something, sing or talk, but get my mind away from the sea and the easy way out.

Nearly always we were helped away from morbid thoughts by the weather, and when again it became stormy, *Gilca*, without outriggers (we had had to chop them off), bobbed like a cork. Once we were caught by the wind with the sail up and were compelled to run for nearly twenty-four hours. Racing along with one gunwale under water, Hall and I had to bail for dear life, life that was losing the quality of dear with every minute that passed. But all thoughts of cones of light had been banished. We sat on the windward side of the boat, Jack with his feet on the water tank and the bed-boards below him removed, me in the cockpit, taking turns to dip our bailing tins into the bilge because we dared not lean forward together for fear the boat would capsize. Steering and bailing was a difficult job. We managed to keep the water at approximately the same level but this just kept her floating which was all we were interested in just then. Life had suddenly assumed a preciousness that it had not had the previous day and we were relieved when the wind dropped sufficiently to allow the sail to be hauled down. Hall took over the tiller and I went forward to lower the tattered square sail, as it was essential that we had some sleep. I found I was not strong enough and Hall had to give the sail the initial pull up. *Gilca* was altogether too lively, making it almost impossible for us to stand. We thought this was because the mast was too high rather than our weakness. So, after getting the sail down, we decided that when the sea calmed, we would un-step the mast and cut about four feet off it, in the hope the boat would be more manageable.

The following morning, we woke to a calm, brassy sea without a suggestion of wind. This was the type of weather we wanted for the tricky business of mast cutting. Not being bothered by such mundane things as having breakfast we decided to do the work while it was cool and we still had energy from the night's sleep. The sail was detached and stay wires unlashed from the gunwale fastenings. All we had to do now was lift the mast out of the hole in the thwart. So, with all the energy we possessed Hall and I lifted, wrestled and tugged at that five-inch diameter pole until it was laid floating in the sea with the base securely fastened inboard. Taking turns, we hacked at a point four feet from the bottom and with much laboured breathing eventually succeeded. Hall used the old step as a model and began to make another one on the newly cut end. Many rests were necessary before the work was completed to our joint satisfaction. Then came our greatest trial of the whole voyage. The weather began to change and whereas the sky had been a gorgeous blue flecked with cirrus clouds, it rapidly became overcast, turning the sea to a leaden grey. With only a moment's hesitation we grabbed the 'mainspring of our motor' and tried to rear it by placing the foot in the hole in the thwart. Hall and I lifted at the point of balance. The foot of the mast slipped. We tried again and again until it became obvious we were too weak to lift it high enough to allow the base to enter the hole. The rising sea had spurred us on to do our absolute best, but we had to admit defeat. My chest felt ready to burst and a suspicious taste of blood in my mouth warned me not to strain any longer. Sitting back, gasping and trembling, I thought of the eighteen previous days of starving and, looking at my swollen-eyed friend's wasted body, cursed myself for all the fools in the world for having agreed to un-step the mast.

After an imposed rest, we tried to step the mast again, but it was useless. For three solid hours with an ever-worsening sea we tried to do the impossible. We had not lost hope, but we were worn out. Our undernourished bodies were not up to the task. If the mast was lost, we might as well blow our brains out because nothing could save us. Knowing we had tried every conceivable thing that human beings in our condition could do, we stood clinging to the mast for support, Hall at one side, myself at the other, gasping, trembling and staring. We were beaten, completely beaten, but too tired to move. For a while I watched Hall's face carefully and noticed the look of strain gradually disappear, to be replaced with a shy, inquiring smile. His mouth opened and in a hardly audible voice, he whispered, 'Why not say a prayer, Skipper?' Wondering if I understood right, I looked at him in amazement while he nodded his head slowly to show he understood the strangeness of his request. In a trembling voice I answered him, 'We've tried everything except that; it can't make matters any worse.' Closing my eyes, I moistened my cracked lips in an effort to speak more clearly and began to pray. 'Almighty God help us and give us strength to re-step the mast. We've done all we can and now we ask for Divine assistance, for Jesus Christ's sake, Amen.'

My prayer may seem funny to some people and they might find excuses for what happened and say we had time to regain our second wind. Perhaps the praying was just the rambling of someone slightly unbalanced through starvation. Perhaps, but believe me nothing was less funny. We were absolutely and utterly helpless. Neither of us was what people would call religious and I am sure Hall's suggestion to pray was purely a brainwave. I had stated our case as clearly as possible. I looked at the rising sea and silently supplemented my spoken appeal to the Divine Creator for His help. The prayer lasted about half a minute and with a 'Now let's try' to Hall, we picked up the mast as though it weighed ounces instead of pounds and re-stepped it. Hall's red beard opened in an unbelieving smile and my grey one followed suit as we automatically turned to face the wide expanse of ocean to mutter our very grateful thanks.

We then took a reef in the sail by rolling up the boom, allowing us a sail area of about 120 square feet. This size we found could be pulled up or lowered by either of us individually. With short ends of telephone cable, we repaired the sail and again turned *Gilca*'s bow towards Australia. We felt new beings and Hall demonstrated his new lease of life by trying to sing a song entitled 'My Hat's on the Side of my Head'. It was a miserable croak, but we were happy.

As I have previously mentioned, the only book we had on board was the Bible, and due probably to the mast incident it became our custom at two o'clock each afternoon to read a chapter from the New Testament. Unfortunately my sight had deteriorated to such an extent that I could not see the print and Hall had to do the reading. He read clearly and slowly, occasionally putting down the book while we debated the problems that confronted the disciples, being particularly interested in the voyage during which St. Paul was wrecked. I had never read the Bible before and neither, I think, had Hall. Coming to the end of the chapter, he would always finish with 'Here endeth the reading of the Lord's holy word'. The Bible would then be carefully wrapped up and placed in the wooden safe along with the charts, and our undivided attention would once more be given to sailing.

30 June dawned a glorious sunny morning with just the right amount of wind for splendid sailing, provided we had been travelling in the opposite direction. This was our 'deadline' day, the sixty-first at sea and our twentieth without food of any kind. Opening the safe, I took out the chart, which showed we were still 200 miles from North-West Cape. We felt it strange that no patrolling aircraft had been sighted and we were disappointed as we had hoped to be picked up before now. It was obvious we could not make Australia against the south-east winds and it was also horribly clear we could not last much longer without food. There was only one hope left and that was to turn and use the wind, making for the eastern tip of Java or the island of Bali as according to the wind chart the current set in that direction; ironically it was also the old sailing route to Japan. Discussing this matter, we agreed, but this time very, very doubtfully, that we would try to hold out without food for another ten days, which was my estimated time to reach Java. There we hoped we could ship a hundred coconuts and again try for freedom but next time for Africa. Our motto of 'Australia or sink' had regretfully to be abandoned and cursing all aircraft for not spotting us we put about and laid a course north and east towards the enemy's outstretched arms.

## Chapter 6

# Back to The Enemy

It is difficult to describe our feelings and to say we felt disappointed would be as inaccurate as to say we were angry. A kind of fatalistic indifference to whatever might happen to us is nearest the truth. Sailing in the wrong direction could not be avoided, so there was no reason to chastise ourselves for doing it.

We had lost weight at an alarming rate during the twenty days' fast and with knee and elbow joints badly swollen, we looked pitiable. To all intents and purposes our race was run. We were doomed men and whether we could survive another ten days of starvation was doubtful. As if to atone for her slow progress on the outward journey, our small craft simply tore through the water, which made us regret not having sailed west from Enggano. The direction of the wind having remained constant, we estimated it would have been possible to cross the Indian Ocean within forty days and our troubles would have been over, added to which we would have achieved something instead of doodling about in the Timor Sea.

Long periods of silence reigned between us. Then a low burring sound forward attracted my attention. I became petrified as I saw beneath the boom a seagull hovering with fast-beating wings about a foot above the bowsprit. A quick glance towards Hall told me of his amazement too. We dared not utter a sound for fear of frightening the bird away. So there *was* something else in all this wide space besides ourselves! Something other than sharks! It took several seconds before my numbed brain registered that this white-feathered object represented food and I had to do something to get it. My trembling hands crept inch-by-inch to the chart-box where I kept my revolver, fortunately oiled and cleaned. Silently opening the lid, I gripped the weapon, lifting it noiselessly from among a conglomeration of things. I looked at Hall and he nodded a silent 'Good hunting'. The bird rested some ten feet from where I was seated, but the hazard to be overcome included getting off the loose bed boards without making a sound and crossing four feet of no man's land to the mast, all in full view of the quarry. In years gone by, I had had considerable experience of big-game hunting in the Sudan, and I now brought this experience to bear with exaggerated care as I set out upon the longest trek of my life. Both our lives might depend upon my marksmanship.

Turning its head from side to side, the gull seemed satisfied with its security and started to rub with its beak under one wing, then under the other. I felt my barefooted way across that vast four feet of space. Halfway across, the bird turned and looked full at me. Remaining absolutely still, except for my flying hair and beard, I was examined intently, then it resumed grooming. Cautiously moving forward again, I finally reached the five inches of cover given by the mast. The 'great desire' sat perched on the bowsprit four feet beyond. With infinite patience and caution I raised my revolver inch-by-inch to the firing position and took a bead on the gull's shoulder. Gripping the butt of the weapon with my right hand, my left pinned it to the mast to stop my trembling. Taking a deep breath, I squeezed the trigger gently and began to think the striker would never work. My eyes began to water. The grey and white target appeared to become indistinct as though I was looking through a pane of untrue glass. Just when I thought I would have to wipe my eyes and take another breath, the weapon fired and the gull left the bowsprit. My heart seemed to have stopped beating until through tiny slits my eyes telegraphed the joyful message to my brain that in the shoulder of the bird was a red hole about the size of a sixpence and the bird was falling into the sea two feet from the boat. With the report of the revolver followed by the disappearance of the bird the tension snapped and as silence was no longer necessary, I shouted, 'Jack, get it!' *Gilca* was moving at a decent speed and we had to move rapidly otherwise the sharks might beat us to it. Hall got the seagull in with one of the basket oars we had used on our way over to the islands from Padang. Shaking hands, we chuckled with delight and were half-demented over our success, each of us holding and fondling the bird to convince ourselves this was no dream.

While Hall grabbed the axe to decapitate the gull, I produced an enamel mug, thrust the neck of the headless bird into it and pumped it dry of blood. Unable to contain ourselves any longer, we added fresh water with just a dash of seawater for flavouring and enjoyed a mugful of the most delectable drink in the world, at any rate in our world, which we agreed was 'Grade Double A'. The physiological fact of giving ourselves a blood transfusion was sufficient to prevent us from tearing the bird to pieces then and there. I sat watching, mentally enjoying my portion, while Hall sharpened the knife on the axe-head before dissecting our lunch. No plucking was to be done; that process was much too slow. Hall said skinning the gull reminded him of many ducks he had handled in the same way. There was no fish in the bird's gullet but that did not worry us. We were completely satisfied. Here was the thing we craved for most, food, and while sweetbreads and legs were being dropped in our respective enamel mugs, it suddenly dawned on me this was not the only bird in the world, and it was possible another miracle might happen. Turning my watering mouth from the mug, now full of choice luscious meat, I deliberately cleaned the revolver in case another gull should land.

We chatted away trying to calculate the additional sustenance we would get from the meat. We agreed that ten days' additional starving could certainly be accomplished with such a base to work from. A meal of such magnitude seemed unbelievable, and although terribly hungry, neither of us ate one single piece of flesh until the division had been completed. Then Hall put down the knife and said, 'Let's go, Skip.' The serious business of eating had to be given priority. The tiller was lashed and whether *Gilca* drifted ten miles off her course mattered not one iota. We sat one on each side of the water tank steadily chewing the exquisite raw flesh and looking at each other with smiling eyes, for the time being utterly content. This was the first food we had eaten for twenty long days. Six hours later, in the soft light of evening, we were still chewing bones to destruction, in the process of which I broke two teeth off my dentures but such a minor problem did not worry me.

Our feast over, we felt life was well worth living. The flesh of the bird had been beautifully tender and, most surprisingly, did not taste of fish. Cleaning up the mess and signs of our orgy, we threw the feathers overboard and settled down with renewed vigour to the task of reaching land. I suggested we were probably nearer Java than I thought, using as argument the now-consumed seagull. The bird had obviously come from the land but neither of us knew how far they could fly. Nevertheless, we were prepared to believe land was not far away and all-in-all it was a night of great rejoicing.

Just before dawn the weather changed and great gusts of wind threatened to carry away the sail, which was hurriedly lowered and made secure. The rope was paid out over the bow and *Gilca* bided her time riding head to sea.

Tired though we were we realised we must take advantage of the rain to fill the water tank and the old procedure of bailing was started until the water was voted fit to drink. The tank was half-empty and to insert some twenty gallons by a pint mug through a four-inch hole which kept bucking about was a long and laborious operation. There was no reason for either of us to stand a watch as the boat was riding to the sea anchor. We lashed the tiller firmly and lay down upon sodden blankets, trying to get some warmth into our numbed bodies and praying for the dawn and sunlight. Neither of us could sleep so we chatted about the pleasurable things of life, and again, when we thought nothing could surprise us, there came a surprise. We were electrified, as in the waning light came a weary messenger from the sky and we saw another seagull on the bowsprit. As I felt for my revolver another wave came, a different one this time. It was a wave of compassion for the poor creature that was obviously as tired as ourselves. It had perhaps battled against the storm as long as we had, but if I could shoot straight it had to die and I hoped that gallant bird would never know. Into the pouring rain I went, slowly and carefully, and repeated the tactics of the previous day. Five minutes after it had landed, the gull lay dead in the boat. Hungry as we were, we were too tired to prepare it for eating so we contented ourselves by chopping off its head and drinking the blood. In pumping the bird dry, several squid came out of its gullet and we ate them with relish. The body was laid on the water tank and, pulling a corner of the blanket over our heads, we again tried to go to sleep until the water washing about in the bilge should wake us by splashing through the slats we lay on.

I remember thinking this was to be my first good night's sleep on the long voyage. Being too exhausted to eat yet knowing that tomorrow's breakfast was waiting kept my subconscious mind clear of the horrible fantasies which had plagued me night after night during the twenty days of enforced starving. I had dreamt of tables stretching away to infinity in long, low buildings situated always in beautiful grassy meadows peopled with the most generous and kindly folk. From tables piled high with luscious food these dream-folk would press upon me great pieces of cheese and steaming mugs of cocoa, which nearly made me choke as I smelled the food. Hall and I compared notes about our dreams and found they were practically identical. We were allowed to select and handle any food we wanted but as soon as we lifted some tasty morsel to our lips the dream vanished, and we woke. With aching heart and bones, we tried hard to sleep again and recapture the scene of plenty, swearing on our honour to the kindly dream-folk we would not try to eat if only we could just look at the food. It was horrible torture and I think at this time we were both very near to death.

Rising somewhat refreshed from the sleep of exhaustion, I was pleased to see the morning was fine and clear because this meant the sodden smelly blankets could be dried. There on the tank lay our decapitated breakfast, the most welcome sight I have ever seen. That bundle of feathers was beyond price; all the Rothschild millions could not buy it. I pulled the blanket tightly round me to keep out the chilly morning air and perhaps weariness overcame me, for how long I do not know, but something in my brain was trying to connect the events of long ago with today. Surely today was 2 July, and if so, then this was the anniversary of my wedding day and I had not sent my wife a bouquet of red roses as I always did. I looked round to find some way to solve the problem, when my eyes focused upon a seagull perched upon the bowsprit. Once again, I repeated my killing routine. The revolver cracked and in the short time that the bullet was crossing the space from mast to bowsprit, I realised what a fool I had been not to wake Hall, as the gull might easily drop into the sea and float past the boat before I could grab it. But the Fates were kind and number three bird fell into the boat. Hall sat up as though I had shot him. His eyes travelled from the bird in my hand to the one on the tank, and as I laid them side-by-side, he was already groping for the axe to behead the latest arrival. We sipped the blood as one would drink morning coffee, while Hall skinned our breakfast with now and again a covetous glance in the direction of our supper.

The situation was rapidly improving and if we could only carry on like this, we might put on a little more flesh by the time we reached Java. Breakfast finished, our attention had to be given to sailing as a brisk breeze sprang up. This made a real joy of the work. The blankets were put out to dry and very nearly lost in the strong breeze but no other incident happened. Our shadow, the sharks, still followed and we were quite used to them by this time. That night we ate our third bird and hoped we should soon be able to shoot another, but we were doomed to disappointment. The only bird we did see was an albatross, hovering high in the heavens. How we wished for a rifle! An albatross might contain the soul of a dead mariner but that would not have stopped us from killing it.

This life, if it was life, seemed to consist of guiding *Gilca* through darkness over a sea of darkness with spells of oblivion in between. Nine such periods, which represented days, passed by and still no bird arrived. In thirty days, we had had three seagulls between us and now we were more dead than alive. During these nights, I used the time by putting my arms on the tiller bar, leaning my head on them and keeping my eyes fixed on the compass which I could hardly see. Hope began to fade and each morning I saw the look of hopelessness on my friend's face. Handing the tiller to him this morning, I reminded him that tomorrow we should see land. It was the only cheerful thing I could think of. When tomorrow arrived, the tenth day after turning the boat back to Java and our seventieth day since setting out from Enggano, I spent an hour carefully scanning the horizon as I felt sure we must be near land. Turning to Hall I had to admit no land was visible but perhaps it was covered by the haze though neither of us could see any haze. What excuse *could* I give? The air was as clear as crystal, there was no land, and we both thought there never would be any for us. Perhaps in another day or so it would not matter. I did not like Hall's morose silence and tried to get him to give a reason why no more gulls had come our way. For a little while we talked about why the birds were frightened. Then not another word would he say except, 'Leave me alone, Skipper, I'll get over it.' These nine extra days of starvation seemed to be getting him down more than the full twenty days before, though I realised we had had a good base from which to start earlier. The awful gnawing at our vitals was now almost beyond bearing. Somehow we got through another day, and still there was no sight of land.

Our buttocks were so thin and bony it was impossible to sit for long at the tiller even on a folded blanket, and so, as the breeze was constant and from the same quarter, the rudder was lashed. Dragging the thin, miserable things which used to be my legs over the thwart I stood clinging to the mast to scan the horizon. This was about 1 pm. Suddenly something made me turn around. Perhaps it was the wind or perhaps a small noise, but there was Hall feeling in his haversack. When he withdrew his hand, it contained his revolver, which I knew to be loaded. The look on his face told me what he was thinking and exactly what he was going to do. We were in a very tough spot and I too had wondered if it was not the best way out. Still, in an hour a bird might come and perch on our bowsprit or we might sight land. A thousand reasons flashed through my mind why it was the wrong way as I clambered back and came up beside him and placed my hand on the weapon. I said one word: 'Jack'. We looked hard at each other for a moment, then he said, 'It's all right, Skipper, I'm not going to do that.' The tension between us for the past three days was over. He climbed into the tiller cockpit and I followed to see what he intended to do. He fired at a large fish that appeared to be about three feet below the surface. Nothing happened, so he fired again but the fish swam along quite undisturbed. Then placing the revolver barrel in the water, he fired twice in quick succession. There was a loud detonation and I saw Hall's hand jerk up. The barrel was split along its length, enough for us to see the two bullets jammed up one against the other. I thanked heaven my revolver was still in commission. On looking into the water, we could see the fish swimming along as unconcernedly as ever, while we had lost a revolver and four valuable rounds of ammunition.

We had previously said how grand it would be if we only had a box of hand grenades and Hall apparently tried to make his pistol function like a grenade, with disastrous results to the pistol. I could understand trying this method or any other method that might get food. A few more days of this starvation and I doubt if we should have had sufficient strength to skin a seagull had we been lucky enough to get one.

Two very long days later, I managed to shoot another bird and, needless to say, we devoured it ravenously. It was a particularly small gull and merely whetted our appetite. A shark was now following the boat. If we could get it to come close enough, there was a possibility of shooting it. This would provide our bare cupboard with food for days. The sail was lowered, and the shark gained on us, but the big fish never came nearer than twenty yards. So I fired, hoping for a lucky hit, but it did not seem to be affected. It was only after the third shot that it turned away and left us. We were convinced it had been hit and badly wounded so the sea-anchor rope was put over in the hope that within an hour or so it would come floating, belly up, to the surface. I remember having read in some book or other that dead sharks did this kind of thing, but it may have been whales or crocodiles.

After searching the water for three hours in the hope that the shark would turn up, we concluded it was not dead and reluctantly got under way again. While Hall steered, I cleaned the revolver and prepared to load it ready for use. The ammunition was kept in our respective haversacks, and when turning them both out I found the combined result was one last round. I silently damned Hall for firing at the fish and damned myself for the shark-shooting episode but realised that all the condemnation in the world would not bring back the ammunition. We had been fools in anything but a paradise and it seemed we should have to pay the bill sooner than expected, though the creditor had been exceedingly generous and the account was long overdue.

I lay and wondered why land had not shown up if we were in the position shown on the chart. The awful knowledge began to dawn upon me that we were lost and all I could do was to set a straight course north and east and say nothing to Hall. With these thoughts chasing each other round in my brain, my emaciated body finally took charge and unconsciousness crept over me, the sleep of exhaustion bringing me another fantasy of food.

During the early hours, I woke and looked up at the sky. The darkness of night at sea always amazed me as it was possible to see anything in the boat at any hour of the night. My eyes travelled round and came to rest on the mast, which seemed to have become longer. I began to wonder if

I were still asleep as on the top sat a seagull, or a ghost of one. Daring to look away, I looked at Hall and touched him ever so lightly. He woke up and I whispered, 'Look on the mast.' We rolled back our blankets like automatons, rose together, and with a tap on my chest and a quick pantomime, I indicated that I, being lighter, would climb up the mast. Hall nodded. We felt we dare not talk. The boat was swaying, and I had difficulty in getting started with the climbing. Standing on the thwart together, I stretched as high as I could and gripped the mast, while Hall pushed like a Trojan. Then near the top I stretched out an arm and measuring the last few inches, put an additional spurt into my climbing. With fingers extended, I gripped the bird's legs. Nothing could have made me release the grip I had on that bird; though it pecked my hand unmercifully I felt they were mere kisses. We had got another meal. Making our way to the tiller cockpit, the bird's head was cut off and our usual procedure gone through. The rest of that night was spent in an orgy of feeding. It was a regular bloodbath and we were happy again, particularly because we had proved that seagulls could be caught by hand.

I am not quite sure whether it was the 15th or 16th of July that was a great day, but I do know that at 6.20 am our sail was down, with Hall ready to move into position at the slightest sign of our feathered friends. For the moment we sat and chatted, every minute searching the sky for a sign of their coming. In all, eight birds were caught that day. We skinned them all and ate such dainties as the liver, sweetbreads and so on straightaway. The minor problem of how we were to keep them confronted us. Some were placed in brine, while the rest were hung up under the canvas awning to become 'high' to vary the flavour a little.

Our joy and gratitude could not be measured. Even *Gilca* seemed to sail better and the crew's morale was one hundred per cent. We became magnanimous and even allowed birds to land without trying to catch them, chiefly it must be admitted because we wanted them to get a feeling of security, hoping this policy would pay big dividends when the larder became depleted again.

It was fortunate we had so much food on board, as the night brought the end of the long spell of fine weather and foam-topped waves came crashing into the boat once more. The wind reached hurricane force and even our canvas awning was nearly carried away. The sea anchor had been put over the bow much earlier and we concentrated on bailing. Hour after hour the work continued until we were so tired that we reached the mechanical state we had experienced previously.

This storm seemed worse than the others, maybe because we had become weaker. On the third day of the storm we were so weary that we agreed to let the boat fill with water before starting to bail her and take the risk of the odd wave swamping us. In this way, we had some rest with the appropriate risk because if we shipped a heavy sea when the boat was full, this book would never had been written.

## Chapter 7

# An Ocean Without Shores

.

The storm petered out about 20 July on our eighty-first day at sea. My estimate of ten days to Java was apparently far out but still I plotted our course 'that should have been' and each day's sailing was recorded on the chart and in our logbook. The gulls were becoming much scarcer now; one in three days was our average catch. We seemed quite healthy but horribly thin and next to food our great desire was to sleep.

We kept to a north-easterly course, and according to the plotting on the chart we should arrive in Surabaya about the middle of the afternoon, having sailed completely across Java. We both realised we were completely lost, and our only hope lay in keeping a straight course. Neither of us was unduly worried about our position. We should not have minded being in the middle of the Pacific Ocean, for we had absolute faith in our little craft. It was the food problem that worried us and it was so acute that it overshadowed the anxiety about being posted missing. The War Office's usual six months was nearly over and here we were 'serving our time in sail' still free but helpless prisoners. What a paradox!

On 1 August, Bank Holiday, we fortunately caught an adult seagull and another small black bird. So everything was rosy once more, except that the jack-knife was lost. Hall had gathered up the feathers and heaved them over the side, neither of us realising the knife had also gone.

The next day dawned with hardly a ripple on the ocean and not a breath of wind to fill the slanting sail. The sun climbed the heavens while we searched vainly for sight of land or a bird but never again did a seagull land on our boat nor did we even see one. In all, we had eaten some sixty of these birds and to them we undoubtedly owed our lives. We also discussed Captain Bligh quite a bit and felt sure we had now been at sea nearly as long as he had. Little did we realise that the *Bounty's* men had made their historic journey in only forty-eight days.

Day after day that same hateful sea remained. We began to wonder whether the doldrums had moved from the Pacific to the Indian Ocean and wished a storm would spring up to relieve the monotony, but there seemed little hope of that. Having talked about everything, we lapsed into silence, just watching, waiting and starving. To shut out the brassy glare of the sun's reflected light we spent most of the time lying down with a corner of the blanket over our eyes. This period of total abstinence from food seemed very much worse than the previous ones. It was obvious we had at last reached breaking point and quiet sobs from the direction of Hall's blanket brought me out of my stupor to give him a few words of encouragement to which he replied, 'Leave me alone, Skipper. I'm in one of my moods again. It will soon pass off.' Poor devil, his large young body must have craved food even more than mine and heaven knows I would have given anything for a good square meal.

The seventh consecutive day of starvation dawned and the sun rose on our hundredth day at sea. Uneasily we gazed at the horizon through still swollen eyelids. There was no sign of any change in the weather and we were destined to spend yet another day in this glaring circle of water. To make sure there was no sign of land, I crawled off my bed and stood by the mast, searching the horizon, but in vain. I turned and was about to go back to my bed, when between the coils of our sea anchor rope, I spied a fish about nine inches long. Gazing for a moment, I stooped and picked it up and found it was partially decomposed. It was a flying fish that had apparently hit the sail a couple of days ago and dropped back into the boat without our seeing it. Rotten though it was we shared it and then I went forrard again, searching under the rope, hoping there might be more.

I spent the whole morning looking for land, seated up forrard, if one can get forward in a boat seventeen feet long. At about 11.30 Hall came clambering to where I was sitting, and with parted lips and shining eyes, excitement written all over his face, he leaned over me and in a tense whisper said, 'Skipper, at the back of the boat is a tortoise, like one of those things you have in the garden.' Realizing he meant a turtle, I got off the thwart and as quickly and quietly as possible, we went aft, four very bony legs clambering over beds and into the cockpit. It was quite a homely looking creature, but not knowing how turtles reacted to human beings, I was afraid it might dive beyond our reach if I spoke aloud, so I contented myself with a quiet 'Okay, Jack, let's get it.' I wondered what damage the thing might do to our hands with its parrot-like beak. Curiosity did not deter us however. Hall took the right-hand and I the left-hand flipper. In two shakes an eighteen-inch turtle was lying on its back in the bilge. With one blow of the axe Hall beheaded it and then began chopping out the belly skin.

Hall got the 'lid' off and exposed a quantity of grey spongy matter. The liver and other oddments we ate immediately, but the grey meat we rationed, considering it should last for two full days, though we could easily have eaten the lot then and there.

On August 9, the turtle was finished apart from the shell and we cast around for something more to eat. The hard belly skin or shell of the turtle was chopped up. We sucked pieces of it and tried chewing it but found it impossible to swallow. A fin cutting the water near *Gilca* set us wondering if it would be possible to get the shark into the boat. For days, it had circled us and at times had been so near we could have leaned over the gunwale and touched it. Had we had any ammunition, it would have been a simple matter to have replenished our larder. It appeared half-grown, about four feet long, and would be food for many days. Waving a piece of cloth about in the water, we finally enticed it to come near enough for me to grab one of its lateral fins and Hall the other. With his other hand, Hall picked up the axe and chopped at the shark's back, hoping to injure its spine. The blade cut deeply into the flesh, leaving a light grey wound. It must have become annoyed, as it began lashing its tail. Realising one good lash would tear the thing from our grasp, I took the axe from Hall and aimed a blow at its head with all the strength I possessed, hoping to puncture the brain. This last effort caused it to leap partly out of the sea and, crashing into the rudder, smashed it and tore free from our grasp. Stretching outboard, I aimed a final blow at its disappearing head and because my hands were wet the shaft slipped through my fingers and the axe was lost. Knife gone, axe gone. Here was a pretty kettle of fish and yet no fish. Fortunately we had a hammer and with it we completed repairs to the rudder for the third time. The shark hunt had been very exciting and at one stage of the fight we had nearly pulled it into the boat. Had Hall aimed his original blows at the monster's head instead of wasting his strength trying to injure its spine, we might have captured it. After this episode, we never saw another shark.

A favourable wind sprang up and for two days *Gilca* made good headway along her north-eastern course but still no land was to be seen. We were most definitely not going round in circles. The chart showed that we had crossed Java and were approaching the island of Ambon. The whole thing had become ridiculous and I stopped plotting and contented myself by studying the wind chart and currents. We were somewhere on the patch of blue, but where? And how far from land? We had no food but plenty of rust-coloured water. How long could anyone hold out on water alone?

There could be no answer. Again, silence reigned between us and we sat just staring, steering and hoping, while *Gilca* sailed lazily onward across a sea of burnished gold.

Once, while looking over the side watching beautiful fish gliding beneath the boat, I noticed several barnacles on the waterline. Here was a discovery far more important than a Klondike or a Kimberley. We reached down into the water and cleared off as many barnacles as we could, about half a mug full. They looked rather like whelks and as we pulled them off the boat, a blob of grey camouflage paint came with them. Devouring them, we crunched shell and paint, comparing them to oysters because of their pleasant taste. They proved to be most sustaining, though we did wonder that the crunched-up shells would do to our intestines. It was perhaps this thought, coupled with logic and a streak of caution, that stopped us from clearing the boat of barnacles and eating the lot then and there. Each day we removed a mugful and a week passed before the last of the limpets fouling *Gilca*'s bottom had gone. This was the only food we had been able to get, but both Hall and I suffered no ill effects other than violent diarrhoea, which was probably caused by the paint.

The good weather again deserted us. We were beaten by violent storms. We suffered the tortures of the damned in constant bailing and more maddening bailing. The storm gave us more fresh water and two small flying fish, and as it blew itself out we were overjoyed to find a small bunch of seaweed about the size of a wire scrubber and with the same springy texture. The important thing was that it was edible. As the days rolled by, seaweed became more plentiful and small boughs began to float past. All these things we pulled into the boat and Hall developed a great liking for boughs, while I remained partial to seaweed.

August 1942 was drawing to a close; we had now been at sea 123 days. It seemed that land was a myth, that this really was an ocean without shores and that the whole of our lives had been lived together in this little boat sailing everywhere but nowhere. There was no change except fine weather and stormy weather; always there was the sea and hunger. We had turned *Gilca* round on the sixty-first day, hoping to reach the eastern end of Java in ten days. Then came the twentieth, thirtieth, fortieth, fiftieth, sixtieth day. Would this never end? By all the normal laws we should have been dead long ago. Though we were weak and emaciated, the spark of life still burned within us, and the hope of making the grade we scarcely once doubted.

The following morning, we received a tremendous thrill. Away on the horizon we saw a sail and immediately altered course directly for it. It was sailing in the opposite direction and seemed to be sheering away. Our poor old *Gilca* with her tattered sail could not hope to out-sail the stranger with her beautiful spread of canvas and she finally disappeared over the horizon.

Although disappointed by not making contact with the boat and particularly with the food which must have been aboard her, it gave us hope that we were near land. At any rate, there was someone else on this sea.

Early the next morning we watched the sun's golden rays creeping steadily up behind a cloud and the cloud became a mountain, towering thousands of feet into an azure sky. We remained staring, spellbound! We were satisfied just to look at it and drink our fill of the thing we had craved so long. Land! Land meant food and food meant life.

The sun climbed higher and revealed dark blotches that could be nothing but trees. Wild, excited jabbering broke out between us as we tried to point out things to each other. It was land. We could see it. There could be no mistake about that great mountain. Yet, as we stared, the vision vanished, leaving *Gilca* on an unbroken sea. We knew it had not been a hallucination. For a while the land had been amazingly clear. The knowledge was confirmed as we tried to pull in the rope anchor, only to find it had become fast on the sea bottom. With the hammer, we brayed the rope on the gunwale, as we hadn't the strength to untie the knots which made fast the inboard end round the thwart and mast. For more than two hours we hammered away, wishing we had the axe, but although there was no sign of land, the boat we had seen the day before once more appeared and again we signalled in vain.

About 9.30 am our boat was once more mobile, and with a fair wind *Gilca* made towards the hidden shore, which gradually revealed itself as we approached. What a wonderful sight that land was to our sea-weary eyes! We tried hard to remember the name of the volcano on the island of Bali and we spoke of the good time we might have there, if only the Japanese were not in occupation.

At midday we overhauled a small fishing boat lying low in the water, and as we came alongside I asked the two occupants for food. One of them handed me a bunch of nine bananas, which we divided forthwith. Hall skinned and ate his share quickly, throwing the skins into the sea, while I ate fruit and skins as well. Seeing this, Hall cursed himself for every kind of fool. We were advised to sail for an island we could see fifteen miles away marked by a long, slender lighthouse. The Indonesians told us it was uninhabited. It was named *Tikus* [rat] Island and there were plenty of stores in the building. Seeing we could get no more food from these people, I glanced at the coastline and perceived a town of considerable size. I asked the name of the town and was told it was Bencoolen. Bencoolen. I had a horrible sinking feeling in the pit of my stomach, and I asked if it was really Bencoolen, Sumatra. They confirmed it was and that the Japanese were in control.

Glad though I was to see land, almost any town would have been preferable to this one. Bencoolen was only 120 miles away from Enggano, the island where we had begun our voyage on that far-off day, the first of May! We had accomplished 120 miles in 125 days. Surely an unbeatable record! What a couple of fools we should be thought when taken into a prison camp! It was heart-breaking to think that after all our efforts, we had achieved so little and in the doing of it reduced our bodies to just skin and bone. It might have been worse had we returned to our starting place, Enggano, but not much. We thanked the Indonesians and hoisting our sail laid a course for Tikus Island. Hall and I discussed our rotten luck in making a landfall in Sumatra when we had expected to be somewhere in Java. Nevertheless, our joy was great at having made land at all after such a long time and particularly at the thought of the food stored in the lighthouse. We hoped it might be possible to re-provision *Gilca* before the Japanese knew we were in the area and turn the boat west to Africa. My mind was disturbed with the thoughts of the fishermen and I mentioned this to Hall, pointing out that one of them looked more like an Indian than an Indonesian and that I had noticed the fishing lines round the boat were new ones. I had never known a local fisherman who could afford a complete set of new lines.

These thoughts, however, were quickly driven from my mind by the wind which veered completely round, making it impossible for us to reach Tikus Island that day. Away on the starboard side were some trees which looked like coconut palms and that meant food. So we changed course again and vowed that, come what may, that night we would sleep ashore. We were being driving seawards by the current and to prevent this we sailed south of Bencoolen and parallel to the coast. In the distance the shore appeared to project far into the sea, so that we were sailing into a kind of bay. Later we found that the land we were running parallel to was an island and the imagined bay was miles away. It was doubtful we could make it before dark. We decided to put in to the island and swung *Gilca*'s bows round towards the shore. On both the port and starboard sides heavy breakers were running, but 250 yards straight ahead was an area clear of them. Into the centre of these calm waters we sailed our splendid little craft, Hall steering and I conning the boat in.

About half a mile from the shore I turned to speak to Hall and was amazed to see a wall of water twenty feet high rearing up behind us. I had just time to shout, 'Look out, Jack!' when the water fell, fortunately for us, some three feet from our boat. The force of the breaker carried us shoreward at a terrific pace. With a grin on my face I was about to say, 'This is the stuff – being speeded shoreward by breakers', but on turning was horrified to see another wall of water curling right over us. Had I had the time, I should probably have cursed my luck that I was to drown within sight of land. There was no dodging this one and with a yell to Hall, I went into the water. My lungs felt ready to burst as I rose to the surface, only to see another monster breaker towering high above me. I had just a chance to take a deep breath and dived again, because I knew that if that tremendous mass of water fell on me it would probably break my neck. Again, I came to the surface, to see a piece of *Gilca*'s false freeboard floating past me. Clutching it, I looked round for Hall but saw no sign of him. Our craft had been smashed completely and I was alone among the breakers, a quarter of a mile from the beach.

Swimming harder than I had ever done in my life, I tried to get as far shoreward as I could before having to dive in order to miss the next breaker. Releasing my hold on the plank before diving, it became obvious that I was making little headway. No sooner was I under the water than the undertow caused me to spin like a Catherine wheel head over heels, and when I came to the surface my plank had disappeared. I was afraid of becoming completely exhausted. Diving again, I felt a stinging pain in my leg and putting out my hands I gripped a rock, a pinnacle of coral, to which I clung and found I could put my head above the surface. For five minutes or more I clung to it, not daring to let go. I waited until my breathing became fairly normal. Then I took my chance and stepped forward, found no bottom and started swimming shoreward as fast as I could. I barked my shins on rock but the pool had been crossed and again my grip tightened on the coral to prevent being swept out to sea. There was still no sign of Hall and I cried aloud to God to save him, but even as I spoke I knew that the unfortunate fellow had not the slightest hope in that angry turmoil. Even for anyone who could swim, the odds were twenty to one against, especially for anyone in our physical condition. I was bleeding freely where my body had come in contact with the coral and, half-drowned, I clung to the submerged rock, trying to regain my breath and energy.

Summoning all my courage, I made another effort to reach the beach, and although repeatedly touching bottom, I seemed unable to make any progress because of the undertow. Coming to the surface yet again, I glanced towards the shore to judge the distance still to be covered. Of the many miracles which had been vouchsafed us, here was the greatest. Staggering about on the beach was Jackson Hall! When I put up my hand to let him know I was getting along all right, he cupped his hands round his mouth and was apparently trying to tell me something. Struggling further in the direction of the beach, half-swimming, half-walking, I halted again for a rest. I heard Hall shouting and this time the words came faintly but I grasped the message: 'Crawl, Skipper, crawl!' Only then I realised what was wrong with me. My legs had not been used for so long, plus the weakness due to starvation, meant they were not strong enough to carry the weight of my body. So down I went on my knees, head underwater, and crawled along on the bottom, coming up only for occasional breaths. When I was twenty yards from shore, Hall staggered into the water and helped me to the sandy beach. He too, I noticed, was bleeding where he had caught the coral but his smiling face and shining eyes showed me that none of his wounds were serious. Here was the end of the grade. We'd made it, but only just.

I crawled up the warm, sandy beach completely naked except for my ring and wristwatch, which I noticed was still ticking merrily away with the fingers pointing to 3 pm. I mentioned the time to my friend, who was staggering about in search of large pebbles with which to kill some of the myriads of small crabs which infested the beach. He cut a quaint figure in his ragged 'shore-going kit'. Somehow, he had saved his shirt; otherwise, except for a ring, he was also naked.

It was a coincidence that our journey should have finished exactly to the minute because it was precisely at this time on 1 May that we had set sail from Enggano 125 days before, according to the logbook which now lay at the bottom of the sea, the present date according to our reckoning being September 3.

We caught some of the small crabs and, crushing them between the pebbles, ate the choicest morsels. After eating several I became careless and placed a bit of gall bag in my mouth, which made me retch violently. Crabs held no further attraction for me and I got on my feet and made a few erratic steps towards some seaweed. Completing a late lunch, I returned to the crab-slaughtering department where Hall was still busy. When he had had enough, we both tried walking a little. Staggering across the sand to the edge of the jungle, we came across a small hut built in bivouac fashion.

There were no ends to the building, but it was an ideal place for our night's lodging. Exercising our legs by returning to the water's edge, we were surprised to see a local man coming towards us, looking extremely scared. When a few yards away he flung out an arm and without stopping said, *'Kampong, kampong'* [village]. I shouted to him to come back, but this merely had the effect of making him run faster. Looking at Hall I burst out laughing for there he stood, swaying about, with his fiery red beard fully a foot long, hair down to his shoulders, dressed only in a tattered khaki shirt, trying to balance on his spindly legs. I was a smaller grey edition, with legs even a little spindlier. Both of us with staring, cavernous eyes looking directly at the man was sufficient to set him off at a fast trot as though all his ancestors were after him. Full of seaweed and crab, we returned to the shelter to sleep off the excitement of the day and especially the final battle with the sea.

When I awoke, it was dark and perishingly cold. Outside it was raining and blowing through the open hut with great force. Hall woke up and he too was shivering with the cold. After covering ourselves with sand, we slept again. At 5 am, however, we were so cold in spite of the fact the rain had stopped, that we decided to try to walk towards the village. We tottered along the beach and near a large iron buoy that had been washed ashore we came upon a pool of brackish water. We drank with relish and rejoiced at our good fortune. Then we had even better luck, for behind a piece of rotting timber I found a coconut half-embedded in the sand. We battered it on the buoy until the husk was stripped and then with a large pebble, cracked the nut to find it in perfect condition. We took an hour to eat our breakfast, by which time the sun was beginning to warm the air, making sitting in its light a pleasure. However, this was not getting to the village or to real food, so we hobbled along in the footprints of our frightened informant. About 8 am we saw five people on the beach in the distance coming towards us.

When the five Indonesians came upon us, one of them produced two pairs of dirty shorts and requested that we put them on. Apparently, the man we had seen the night before had reported to the villagers our state of nudity, but had not taken in our physical condition, as my questions about how much food they brought with them merely produced a negative answer. I cursed them for dolts and two of them were instructed to return to the village at once and bring food quickly while we staggered along in their wake.

The men appeared friendly and willing to help, provided we could pay, and I struck a bargain with the eldest of the trio agreeing to part with my watch for a boat and provisions. Nearly all their talk centred on the Japanese of whom they were mortally afraid, but the old man told me that there was an astounding number of fifth columnists among their own people. They had to be very careful who they spoke to, as many strangers visited their village from an adjacent camp where the Japanese had a task force of 5,000 locals working on the construction of an aerodrome. I could get no sense out of the old man when I questioned him about the work. He seemed frightened and sorry he had even mentioned the subject. He would not give me any idea of the distance we were from the aerodrome. The only thing he did tell me was that we had landed on Pulau Bayar [payment island].

During that long walk, we came on bits of poor *Gilca* strewn along the beach and the Indonesians pounced on the debris in the hope of finding something of value. They were particularly interested to know whether we had had revolvers but these were at the bottom of the sea or at least I hoped so and I felt no compunction in telling them we had not had revolvers, though I expected every time they swooped on *Gilca*'s remains to see one of them emerge carrying the wooden safe in which the weapons were kept. Fortune favoured us, however, and splintered timber was their only reward. We had to be 'nice' to these people because unless they helped us, our hopes of freedom were as completely smashed as the boat.

Even with frequent rests, we were terribly exhausted and silently cursed the men for not having had the common sense to bring something to eat with them. It was not until noon that those who had been sent for food returned with two woefully small bundles wrapped in banana leaf. We grabbed the packets and tore them open, to find rice in one and wood potato in the other. We ate ravenously and after the meagre lunch, we continued our weary way towards the elusive village over sand so hot that to our bare feet it felt like white-hot metal.

Incapable of enduring the agony of walking any longer, we sat down in the shade. While we were resting, a well-dressed Indonesian in European clothes, including collar and tie, emerged from the trees a little way ahead. The attitude of the men immediately stiffened, and they started to give orders to us to hurry up. I asked them why they were afraid of this fellow, but they did not answer. In fact, the only result was to cause the 'dressed one' to walk towards us and call the eldest man aside. After a little mumbling and nodding, the old man returned and instructed his companions to help us to our feet and get us moving again. The 'fashion plate' walked in front until we arrived at the path where he had appeared. Here he told me we had arrived at the village and that he had given instructions we were to be given food. So saying, he walked off along the beach while we entered the path

*Above left*: Captain C.O. 'Mick' Jennings, R.E.

*Above right*: Bombardier Jackson Hall, Anti-Tank Regiment.

*Above left*: Margery Jennings (née Hellewell) in Accra, Gold Coast.

*Above right*: Mick in the Great War in Mesopotamia (1917–18), Royal Engineers. He was 17 or 18. Didn't see a lot of action – ate oranges and learned Arabic, which is why he was posted to Sudan later.

*Above left*: Mick, now a surveyor, in Cairo during the 1920s.

*Above right*: Mick in the 1920s.

Mick at Cairo Zoo in the 1920s.

Mick hunting hartebeest in Sudan (1924–27). He shot meat for the Sudanese – they only had spears so appreciated his contribution. 'Another hartebeest with Lombie Womuryi (sp?) and COJ – the latter playing the devil (as usual) with Suleiman for not holding the camera right.'

*Right*: Hunters in Africa, 1920s.

*Below*: PWD Office, in Accra, Gold Coast. Mick's office was on the ground floor on the right; the Riley (1927–30).

*Above left*: Mick the postie, Accra (1927–30); heavily reliant on parcels from England.

*Above right*: Margery reading the mail with Smut, who had been given to Mick and Margery on their wedding day. He was so-called because he rolled in the coal cellar one day. He kept Margery company when Mick was off surveying for weeks at a time and went with them later to Malaya. Mick bred wire-haired fox terriers in Kuala Lumpur; later when they moved down to Singapore in 1941–42, Smut came too. Just before the Japanese invaded Singapore, Mick had him put to sleep, a duty many Europeans had to carry out.

Going on trek in Accra, Gold Coast (1927–30). Tin trunk 'J' for Jennings; Riley under cover behind. 'With the watchman, Thomas the cook, Akotia, Kabielle the dog and our 300 OP petrol lamp.'

Margery, Smut and the Riley, Accra, Gold Coast (1927–30); note running boards and luggage ready to go on trek.

The British denying cars to the Japanese, 15 February 1942, Singapore.(*WW2today.com*)

Japanese cycling down the Malayan peninsula. (*warfarehistorynetwork.com*)

Air raids on Singapore (*Wikimedia Commons*)

Bombing of Singapore, February 1942. (*IWM*)

Civilian and PoW Camps in Sumatra. (*Muntok Peace Museum*)

*Above left*: British troops surrendering on 2 February 1942. (*warfarehistorynetwork.com*)

*Above right*: Allied troops evacuated from Sumatra to Colombo on board HMS *Hobart*, 28 February 1942. HMS *Hobart* evacuating troops to Colombo. (*Photo: RAN, photographer*)

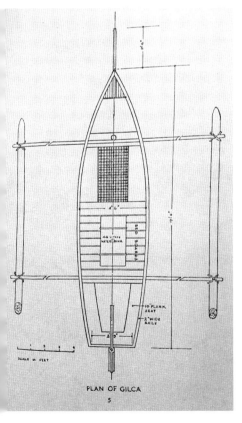

*Above left*: Plan of *Gilca* by COJ.

*Above right*: Sketch of *Gilca* by COJ.

PoW hut, Sungei Ron.
(*pows-of-japan.net*)

Changi Gaol, September
1945. (Australian War
Memorial, 117108)

Changi Gaol interior,
1945.

*Right*: Perhaps this is why so few soldiers talked about it.

*Below*: Lord Louis Mountbatten reading the Order of the Day regarding the Japanese surrender from the steps of the Municipal Building on 12 September 1945.

Singapore – Raffles Hotel: the meeting place.

Evacuation from Singapore.

*Left*: Australian escapees on a raft. (*Australian War Museum*)

*Below*: *Mata Hari*, P&O, on full charter to the Admiralty. (*Muntok Peace Museum*)

*Above*: L to R: Margaret Dryburgh, Norah Chambers, Sister Catharina, Flo Trotter, Berry Jeffrey and Sigrid Stronck. (*Singing to Survive.com*)

*Right*: Attap Barracks Camp, Palembang. Sketch by Margaret Dryburgh. (*Muntok Peace Museum*)

Sketch of Lubbock Linggau Hospital, 1945. Margaret Dryburgh died here shortly after arriving from Muntok. Margery Jennings died here in May 1945. (*Muntok Peace Museum*)

COJ standing second from the left on the SS *Antenor*, returning to England.

*Above left*: Red Cross Officer Ruth Aylwin Stay on the SS *Antenor* (1945).

*Above right*: Showing Lady Gent round Kampong Satu.

Ruth, Mick and wedding party, 16 March 1946. Mick's great friend, Bram, on his right.

Governor General visits Kampong Satu.

MBE ceremony on the Padang, KL.

C.O. JENNINGS, ESQ., M.B.E.

*Above left*: Mick receiving the MBE for his work on Kampong Satu, 1952.

*Above right*: COJ with MBE.

Secretariat, KL, Mick's office is in the closest building.

Motor racing: Mick giving Ruth advice, driving the Black Draught.

Mick book signing *An Ocean Without Shores*, 1950, the story of his escape from the Japanese in 1942.

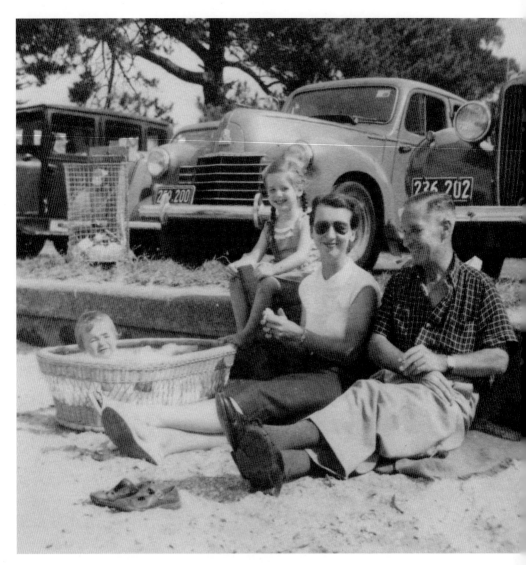

Baby Deb, Sally, Ruth and Mick in Western Australia, 1951.

leading to the small Indonesian-style houses we could see dotted here and there among the trees.

Outside a miserable little shack built on stilts, the guide halted and told us to climb the four-foot ladder and make ourselves comfortable. This was completely beyond our power but with the help of the escort we were dragged and pushed until we were sitting side by side on the open verandah. We could see two women busying themselves on the ground by an open wood fire. All around us and from behind banana palms and gardens of wood potato plants, faces peered at us, but they were afraid to come any nearer.

In a short while, coffee and fried rice were given to us and we were soon asking the women to refill the enamel plates, for the portions originally doled out seemed pitifully small. More coffee and even cigarettes were given to us. What a pleasure it was to feast our eyes on the greenery of the bush instead of the brassy glare of the sea! Turning, I saw three figures coming along a path, dressed in grey-green uniform, armed with rifles with fixed bayonets. Immediately behind them was our 'friend' the Rat, the collar and tie local, who had passed on the information regarding our whereabouts. The uniformed men were Indonesian policemen who quite clearly indicated with the point of the bayonet that it was time we were moving, and quickly. We had no alternative but to obey orders and our original guards helped us get down from the verandah. The policemen told us to walk back to the beach.

Soon we were being goaded along that white strip of burning sand, round headlands and along the shores of bays. It had been 2.30 pm when we left the village and at 4 pm, after falling down several times, I told the guards we could not go any further without a rest. One of them became very truculent and began to jab us with the point of his bayonet. Had we had the strength, we would have attacked the guard and of this I am sure they were aware. Trying to smooth things over, one of them said they had to get back quickly and as it was now 6 pm and there was still a long way to go, we had better start walking again. He saw the surprise on my face at this apparent barefaced lie about the time and then he explained that Tokyo time was two hours ahead of normal local time. The sky had darkened prematurely and, knowing the skies well by this time, I was not surprised when rain began to fall. During the hours that followed, we fell down many times, but each time we were compelled to get up again and march. At last we came to the area being cleared as an aerodrome, and in the darkness we were forced to cross it. Walking along the hot sand had been purgatory but barking our shins on felled tree stumps and trying to extract thorns from our feet while balancing on one insecure leg was absolute agony. The end came suddenly as we came to the sea again where we were bundled into a boat and rowed 200 yards to the mainland. On the way over I looked at my watch and saw it was 11 pm. We had been walking (or rather staggering) on and off since 5 am that morning, a distance we estimated at ten miles and which contained all the tortures of hell.

On reaching the mainland the guards bundled us up a short, steep hill, which nearly finished us off. There we found a road with a British 'battlewagon' waiting and a tall, broad person came up to me whom I could just distinguish from his uniform to be an Indonesian police commissioner. His first remark made both of us jump violently, as he asked, 'Are you Captain Jennings?' When I said yes, he put his hand out and grasping mine, shook it. Noticing I winced, he asked me what the matter was, and I explained how very cold I was. Taking off his big cloak he wrapped it round me, ordering one of his men to do likewise for Hall. This kindness was very much appreciated and when we were put in the car, he offered cigarettes. Hall being a non-smoker did not accept but the cigarettes I smoked were like nectar. Speaking in English, the Indonesian commissioner said he was taking us to the Japanese Residency in Bencoolen. The distance from Pulau Bayar to Bencoolen was about five miles and the commissioner warned us that before entering the Residency, he would be compelled to retrieve the capes, which was done as the car pulled up outside the building, where in an atmosphere of tense and absolute silence we waited for 'His Excellency'. After five minutes or so, a lot of heel-clicking indicated his approach and the rear door of the battlewagon was thrown open to reveal a fat little man swathed in a kimono. Flash lamps were turned on us enabling him to get a better view of his new 'guests'. Satisfied with his inspection, he uttered the single word 'gaol', and turned to enter the most beautiful house he had ever occupied, to the accompaniment of more heel-clicking, saluting and bowing.

The police squad rapidly embussed and again we were on the move, but only for a short time, as the car soon pulled up before a large stone building which the kindly pro-British commissioner said was to be our home. The police helped us get out and took us to the office, where we were treated with the utmost kindness. The dirty shorts we wore were replaced by clean *sarongs* and coats. Tobacco was also given to me from the commissioner's own private supply, and could the Japanese have heard the remarks of these loyal Indonesians they would have had real reason to doubt the success of their New Order in Asia.

While putting on my new clothes, I looked round the office and noticed a large block calendar hung on the wall with the figure six below the month, September. I queried the date and was told that it was correct. Hall and I were nonplussed, as this new date meant that somehow, somewhere, we had lost two whole days at sea and therefore the length of our voyage was 127 days.

Thanking them all for their kindness, we were led across an open yard to a massive iron-barred gate over which an electric light shone, disclosing the white faces of the prisoners behind. Aware that something unusual was happening, they had left their beds and crowded to the gate. With a jingling of keys, the gaoler unlocked it and with a sigh of resignation, Hall and I crossed together the threshold of captivity.

# BOOK TWO

BOOK TWO

*Chapter 8*

# Hospital

The morning came and a breakfast of ground rice and banana was given to us with an excellent cup of coffee. We knew our shrunken stomachs couldn't take much, but the awful empty feeling was almost unbearable. To ease the gnawing ache, I rolled a cigarette and had just lit it when one of the prisoners came in saying the police commissioner had arrived and he (i.e. the prisoner) had received orders to take Hall and me for interrogation. We hobbled to meet him and were put in a taxi and driven to an office near the Residency. We felt very conscious of our shabby appearance as we were led into a room where a Japanese civilian was seated behind a large desk. I was not surprised that he smiled when we entered the room, for the Honourable White Men must have looked very funny indeed, but to give the man his due he treated us with respect, offering us cigarettes and tea. A second person I immediately recognised as the 'Indonesian' fisherman from whom we had got the nine bananas and who had directed us to go to Pulau Tikus. At the time I had been uneasy, thinking he might be Indian. Now I knew the truth. He was a Japanese stained dark to resemble an Indonesian.

The interrogation began and I was surprised we were questioned together, until it became clear he knew the whole story. The officer smiled as he mentioned the Belgians on Pulau Pagai, but I was relieved he did not mention the three soldiers with bad feet we had left there. Perhaps they got away. He made it clear the party who had given themselves up to Marinas on Enggano told them that originally there were two other members. The interrogation officer treated our escapade as a great joke, telling us that no British soldier could get away from *Dai Nippon* [Great Japan]. Although he thought the whole business funny, he nevertheless treated us kindly and with marked respect, allowing us to be seated throughout the interview which lasted two hours, after which we were taken back to the gaol. There we spent the rest of the day in comparative peace, if one ignored the hundreds of questions asked by the Dutch civilians.

The next morning, the interrogation officer again appeared and instructed Hall and me to sit at the foot of a palm tree, when he draped on our respective knees the dirty shorts which had been given to us by the locals just before our capture. He then produced a Rolleiflex-type camera and took our photographs and told us we were to be taken to hospital. A short while after, we got in the taxi and were whisked away.

I looked around at the splashes of colour made by the cannas against the palm fronds waving gently like black silhouettes in the bright blue sky. The sight was wonderful after the monotonous vista of the sea but the sound of surf booming nearby was heartbreaking. It might as well have been a thousand miles away. Within a few hundred feet lay the western seaboard of Sumatra, the gateway to freedom. We had failed once but we knew better this time.

At the hospital, a single-storey brick building, great play was made of having us carried into the ward on stretchers, although we could have walked. In the ward were twenty-six beds, twenty being occupied by natives and the remaining six, Europeans, one of whom was Good, now completely recovered after having had fever and ulcers. He and Thorlby's party had stayed with Marinas for two months before they were taken to Bencoolen. They had then been despatched to Palembang, where there was a British PoW camp.

The ward we occupied had been used pre-war for native patients and the Japanese idea of humiliating the arrogant European was to compel him to live in conditions which previously he had deemed only good enough for coolies. We therefore enjoyed the company of criminals who were ill with malaria and dysentery, while the European members seemed to be either suffering from venereal disease or had sufficient money to bribe the Chinese doctor to allow them to stay in hospital where they occupied comfortable beds and could buy unlimited supplies of food. It was a miserable finish to our voyage on a cruel but nevertheless clean sea.

The next day a barber came to the hospital with instructions to remove our beards and cut our hair. No sooner had this been done than another photographer arrived. The doctor wrote in chalk on a board our names and the treatment we were receiving, and this was placed behind us. Hall was asked to put his arm round my shoulders, leaving a gap between us so that the board with the prescription would come into the picture. The camera was clicked, and the photographer uttered the word *'Domei'* [the name of the leading Japanese news agency]. Then we were left alone to eat the only medicine we ever got, *buboor* [thin rice gruel]. Hall was so hungry that it became his practice to save the coffee grounds and mix them with his rice. We assumed the pictures were to be used as propaganda to prove to the world how kindly the Japanese treated captured British soldiers.

On September 8, we were weighed for the first time and I have tabulated the figures given to me by Hall, who preserved the record all through the days of our confinement. As a gauge to putting on flesh, I would check the size of my ankles. When first admitted to hospital I could easily place my fingers round my ankles and cover the nail of the middle finger with my thumb.

That first night in hospital I felt so weak, and with the strangeness of lying on a mattress and the lack of fresh air, I had only a passable night. Over the next few days Hall and I introduced ourselves to the other Europeans in the ward, one being a chap with a big red beard, Treverrow, a Cornishman and assay master with the Dutch government at a gold mine. Treverrow told us hawkers visited the ward regularly and that if you had money, anything could be bought. Knowing I had no possessions other than my watch and wedding ring, I realised gaining any weight would be a slow process, although Treverrow assured me he would look after me as 'we British need to stick together.' I asked him what the set-up with the doctor was and he explained that as the only doctor in the hospital he was extremely busy and was inclined to let people hang on in the relative luxury of the hospital.

Pointing around the ward, Treverrow introduced me to the other patients. Across from me was an Indonesian, Zainal, a schoolteacher. The next ten inmates were serving sentences for various criminal offences. There were rubber planters, an electrical engineer and more gaolbirds.

Later, Hall brought me a plate of rice and sat on the edge of my bed. We talked over the doings of a momentous day. It seemed ages since our capture.

A little later, Zainal, the schoolteacher in the corner, walked over and in a cultured English accent asked if I would like a cigarette. Of course I was very grateful for the offer and asked him if he had been educated in England. It turned out he had done his degree at Cambridge. Brought to the hospital with malaria when in the area on holiday, he was now stuck waiting for a pass to go back to Palembang. I enjoyed our chat and he was interested in how Hall and I had survived on the boat for so long with so little food. He then intrigued me by confiding there was a collaborator in the ward and to be watchful of my words. He wouldn't elaborate but intimated it was not one of the Indonesians or Dutch. Leaving me pondering this piece of information, he returned quietly to his bed. I was intrigued by the young man. His studiously cautious talk and questions about our voyage made him difficult to place. His keen brain fitted him for a diplomatic career rather than a schoolteacher. Both he and Treverrow undoubtedly possessed qualities of leadership and perhaps their personalities clashed.

Being too weak to stand in line for my meal, I relied on Hall to bring me my plate of food at breakfast time; however, he made no move to help me and I watched as he ran around doing Treverrow's bidding and occasionally glancing over at me.

I began to realise there were several factions and Hall was siding with Trev and his cronies. He left me in no doubt when he told me he was going to be Treverrow's batman, explaining that Good acted as batman for another chap, a giant of a man called Grandos, and the work was a piece of cake. All he had to do was wash Treverrow's clothes and sheets and collect his food. He could eat what his master left. Treverrow had plenty of money and had everybody in his pocket.

Hall's rapid descent into servility surprised me. He had not been servile at sea and neither had he given me the impression of being quite so gullible.

A short while later Treverrow walked over to my bed and suggested I could start to 'pay my own way' as he had spotted my watch and ring, suggesting that things like that were easily convertible as he ran the Black Market in the hospital. Offering me twenty guilders for the pair, he assured me I would have my meals provided regularly with some meat and fish.

I was not impressed and now knew the reason for his false kindness. He wanted my poor belongings. I curtly turned him down explaining the ring and watch were presents from my wife and I was not interested in selling.

I must have drifted off as hours later I opened my eyes to a world that seemed unreal. Shapes and windows and figures appeared untrue, as though seen through thick glass. A tickling on my neck made me put up my hand. It came away wet with perspiration. The pillow was soaked, and I realised I had been out for over thirty-six hours with another bout of fever. A feeling of absolute weakness made me too weary even to think. All I wanted was to be alone, though I was grateful when the dresser turned my clammy pillow.

The next morning, hunger told me I was on the road to recovery. On the locker, a plate with a small white steaming mound awaited me, looking like a snow-covered peak in the light of the morning sun. Through half-closed lids I peered at Hall's bed. It was empty. I glanced down the ward and saw him sitting next to Treverrow, but there was none of the bawdy laughter to which I had become accustomed. Glad to be so much better, I reached for the plate and, putting it on my lap, had a feeling that something was different, something I could not place. The atmosphere in the ward was tense and expectant. What had happened while I was asleep?

Eating what I could of the rice, I put the plate back on the locker. A sudden anger swept through me as my eyes fastened on the untanned skin of my wrist where my watch had been. I looked at the finger on which I had worn my ring; now there was only the tiny pale waist it had made. My precious links with the past had been stolen! As though the realisation of my loss had triggered them, everyone started talking. Curbing my temper, in my helpless state I resolved to use guile. Hall was the weak link in the Black Marketeer's chain, and it was upon him that I decided to play. I called to him, keeping any sign of rancour from my voice and asked him if he would be good enough to wash my plate. As he picked up the plate and turned to go, I asked him quietly if he could ask Treverrow to let me have my watch and ring back.

With a puce-coloured face he said he didn't know what I was talking about and left me as though he were trying to get away from a cobra. As he passed Redbeard's bed, I saw him nod in the direction of the verandah door and a moment later he stepped outside. The rest of the gang rose with pretended casualness and strolled through the same doorway.

Ten minutes later the dresser entered the ward carrying his white enamelled tray. I might have been fooled had not Good followed him in. The little corporal had been one of the satellites who had left by the verandah door. It was patently obvious he had been given instructions to tell the wall-eyed dresser to deal with me. I was to be put to sleep and so prevented from asking awkward questions. The man handed the tray to Good. I made no effort to stop Walleye swabbing my arm. He picked up the syringe, filled it and went through the routine of expelling the air. Then he attempted to lift my arm.

'Not today, "doctor",' I said, drawing away from him.

'But you must,' he replied vehemently. 'It is the treatment!'

'Prescribed by Dr Ho or Dr Treverrow?'

'What do you mean by that remark?' Redbeard and his confederates had re-entered the ward.

'You're a bit early, aren't you?' I replied. 'You haven't given the man a chance to put me out.' Turning to the dresser I added, 'Fetch Dr Ho. We'll find out more about this.'

Walleye raged and fumed, calling me a fool and many unprintable things, working himself into a frenzy until he screamed at me. As he paused for breath, Good, who had not understood a word of what the man had said, pointed to me and yelled, 'Give him the bloody needle! That'll shut his trap.'

'Where are my watch and ring, you rotten low-down thief?' I shouted. Other patients gathered round my bed as I flung the accusation at Treverrow.

He was about to reply, when a loud crash down by the servery made every head turn. In the doorway stood an angry-looking guard. Everyone stood as though turned to stone as he bellowed, *'Kiotsuke!'* [attention] and came slouching towards the crowd. Where pandemonium had reigned only a moment before, soft footfalls could now be heard. Then they stopped. The man glowered ferociously at the circle of awestruck faces and his eyes finally came to rest upon the dresser. The quiet was shattered as he roared out sentence after sentence which no one understood, yet all knew the intent.

Trembling, Walleye held up the syringe. 'He won't let me give him an injection,' he explained in Malay, and pointed to me.

The Jap peered closely at my bared, swollen arm. 'Ah! Plenty injection,' he said sympathetically in English. 'Injection bad, injection good,' he added, which I interpreted as meaning that even if unpleasant, injections do one good.

There were sighs of relief from the patients. The Nip was a softy. Their terror of him departed and they began whispering among themselves. Good, seeking to ingratiate himself, pretended to poke his finger into my arm, saying, 'Injection good, very good.'

'Ya! Very good!' the Jap stressed the word as though giving thanks to the corporal for reminding him of it and, laying his rifle on my bed, he burst out laughing. The crowd joined in. In a flash the scene changed. The soldier's good humour left him as quickly as it had come. A yellow hand grabbed the neckband of Good's cotton coat and an instant later, the upper half of his body was naked. Stark fear shone in his eyes and sweat glistened upon his bald pate.

'Injection!' roared the guard in the dresser's ear. A boot connected with his shin. With a cry of pain, the dresser jabbed the needle without heed into Good's arm. The plunger was almost at the bottom of its stroke when the corporal's eyes closed. With a moan, he slumped to the floor, leaving the dresser stupidly gaping at a syringe that held only half a needle.

With a roar of laughter, the guard yelled, 'Injection, very good!' and put his foot under the inert body to lift it into the aisle. His action said plainly, 'Get this white trash out of here.'

Grandos picked Good up as though he were handling a sack of rice. He needed assistance from no one, but Treverrow seized on a means of putting distance between himself and a Jap who had gone mad. They dumped the NCO on his bed, pretending to fuss around him, while we were being treated to an incomprehensible harangue.

Dismissing everyone, the guard sat on the edge of my bed.

'Injection no good,' he said by way of making conversation.

'No good,' I agreed with a smile.

He examined my swollen arm and looked curiously at the untanned skin that ringed my wrist. 'Watch?' he asked.

'Yes,' I replied, then showed him the mark on my finger where the ring had been.

'Ah! Wifeo?'

Again, I said, 'Yes,' adding, 'me – injection.' Then closing my eyes and simulating sleep, I grabbed at my wrist and finger, trying to convey that my possessions had been stolen while I lay unconscious.

Looking at me through lowered lids, he slowly nodded his understanding.

'This man steal,' I said, pointing to Hall, and added in Malay, '*Churi-churi*' [thief]. Again, he nodded.

The guard rose to his feet and looked at my ex-companion with an expression that was anything but pleasant.

'Watch,' hissed the guard, holding out his palm. Hall's mouth opened and closed, but he made no sound. The next moment a stinging flat-handed swipe knocked him onto his bed. He got up hurriedly to find a hand drawn back for another blow.

'Trev's got 'em,' he squealed. 'Stop 'im, Skip!'

'Nippon,' I called only just in time, and stroked a long imaginary beard. The guard needed no further information.

'Watch!' he roared, beckoning the Black Marketeer.

'Ya, ya! Nippon want good watch.' As he hastened along the aisle, Treverrow drew a timepiece from his pocket and put it into the Jap's hand, smiling unctuously. For a second or two the guard examined it and then held it up for me to see. I shook my head.

There was a shriek as the guard dropped the butt of his rifle heavily upon the assay master's slippered foot. Hobbling with pain, he tried to stand still.

'Watch!' said the soldier again, but this time he said the word softly. If he had seemed dangerous when bellowing, he was deadly when quiet. The thief bowed and hobbled away quickly. With legs wide apart, the Jap balanced on the balls of his feet like a boxer, while his narrowed eyes never left the man who had tried to fool him. His fingers gripped the strap of the watch that Redbeard had tried to pass off on me.

Treverrow came back at a limping double and with a bow gave my watch to the waiting man who for a while compared it with the one he held. He looked at me, I gave a nod of affirmation and without a word he lobbed it into my hands, then turned to deal with the culprit.

The shrewd black-market operator got in first. 'Nippon keep watch,' he said. 'I give present.'

'Presento, eh?' The guard flung the watch onto the concrete floor as though it had stung him. We were then treated to another tirade and again we understood its purport. This incorruptible guard could not be bribed and crushed the remains beneath his heel.

The cunning sycophant stroked his beard and remained unmoved at the sight of the broken gold case. He bowed both to the Jap and to the inevitable, hoping that in the excitement the matter of the ring had been forgotten. However, the guard's memory was not as short as Treverrow would have wished because he came back and held his hand palm upwards just below the mat of red hair. Staking everything on a last throw, the pseudo-Englishman adopted a hurt and questioning expression, having been misunderstood. His action proved he was not the shrewd businessman I had thought him. I doubt whether he knew what hit him, for the guard's hand had moved like lightning from beneath the beard. Trevelyan got up from the floor, bowed, drew a cake of soap from his pocket, broke it and dropped my ring onto the guard's waiting palm.

Dismissing the thief with an *'ush'* [get lost] the friendly enemy whom I decided to nickname 'Inco' threw the ring to me. 'Good!' he said, somewhat savagely as though annoyed with himself for having helped me.

It was strange that this Jap had defended me from my own kind. Outwardly there was nothing to distinguish him from the other guards. He had shown touchiness and violence equally, but only for a reason. Other Japanese would bawl and rave simply because they wanted to frighten everyone. 'Inco', the incorruptible guard, was not deliberately cruel. Even in the Imperial Army, a two-star private could and did smack a one-star man's face for an offence, before either officer or prisoner. Justice may have miscarried on occasion but there was no Orderly Room as we know it hanging over the head of an offender. What was humiliation for us was standard practice to them. Inco worked to the rule with unexpected refinements.

The unpredictable Japanese gave me a smile as if to let me know that he knew what the game was. He turned his back on the ward and sat on the edge of the bed.

Facing me he said, 'My ... father ... officer ... *Shonan.*'

'Your name Shonan?' I asked.

His smile widened as he shook his head. 'Before war ... Singapore. Now ... Shonan.' I nodded and he continued, 'Me University Tokyo ... war ... finish soon ... me go ... home.'

'Good luck!' I replied and was surprised to see him pull from his pocket a small book printed in Japanese, English and Malay.

He thumbed the pages for a while. 'Ah, yes!' He had apparently found the phrase.

'*Arrigato* ... er ... thank you.'

Putting the book away, he looked at his watch as the meal gong sounded. Getting to his feet he gave me a little bow. I returned it in what I hoped was bow perfect. Inco picked up his rifle and sauntered to the servery. There he stood, looking through the hatch, watching the amount put on every patient's plate. It may have been coincidence, but everyone seemed surprised at a larger than usual ration. The dresser made a point of bringing mine. When all had been served, he left the ward.

# Chapter 9

# Heaven Has Curtains

I spent many hours lying in that hospital bed wondering what had turned Jack against me. Why was he so subservient to this Treverrow when he owed him nothing? This was not the man I knew whom I had spent so much time with, in such dire circumstances.

One day my attention was drawn to a conversation in Malay just outside my window. The voices were low and difficult to hear but were discussing the execution next morning of myself and Jack! There was debate as to why the Japs had waited all this time to decide to execute us. One swore that his sister, who was getting married to one of the policemen who delivered us from Serdang, had told him the superintendent had been arrested by the Kempeitai and that an example would have to be made of him. Evidently the superintendent had argued with the Japs and told them it would be murder. It seemed, if this were all true, that our friend who had been so kind to us might be in jeopardy for trying to help us.

The two men continued their discussion about graves being dug at the back of the mortuary, until they had to retreat as they heard Japs coming. A few moments later the hated command *'Kiotsuke!'* [attention] rang out and the patients sprang to attention. There were five Japanese in all, the foremost being the sergeant who had originally brought us in and who was obviously in charge of the party. He halted in front of Hall and me and spoke to the guards, pointing to each of us in turn. I could not understand what he said but he looked delighted. He posted a sentry at the farther side of the glass door and then the party marched out of the ward.

Hall gasped, 'What the 'ell was that about?'

'Your guess is as good as mine,' I replied. 'Perhaps Treverrow should tell you.'

Was this the real thing or did I see Treverrow's finger in the pie? Was it straining coincidence to have been given the whole story, as it were, on a plate, followed by the party of Japs and the posting of guards?

Mealtime arrived and this time Hall collected my plate of rice. He told me he had asked Trev what the Japs wanted but he wouldn't say and gave us both extra rations of fish. If the story were true, this would be our last supper. I ate slowly, trying to sift truth from suspicion. As the lights were turned off, I pondered Hall's ignorance in the matter, which worried me a great deal.

Perhaps I had dozed off for a while, though I could swear I had done no such thing. The events of the day were too sharply defined and unpleasant to sleep on. If the next sunrise were to be the end of my earthly existence, so be it. I was ready and unafraid, though my heart ached at not being able to tell my beloved wife how dearly I loved her.

Then suddenly and with unbelievable clarity I saw a smiling apparition of myself standing in the middle of the aisle, looking objectively at the 'me' who lay in bed. I heard the apparition say: 'Don't worry, for even if they destroy you, you will live, for I am indestructible.'

A great happiness welled up within me and blood pounded in my head, momentarily cutting off my vision. When I could see again, the shadow had vanished, though I knew it was still there watching me. The voice had been so loud and clear.

In my imagination, I could hear the revolving broad-bladed fan in my home in Malaya making a grating noise as it moved out of balance. My wife and I sat beneath it, silently drinking in the beauty of the night as we gazed across the loggia and the moonlit valley to the dark of the distant mountains. Words were superfluous in this perfect harmony of spiritual love.

I rose and leaning over her, kissed her and stepped into the darkness. I walked to the men who waited for me. 'I'm ready now,' I said.

A faint rustling of wings made me look up. There was nothing, nothing at all. I was in a land where it was neither light nor dark. A great feeling of peace stole over me. I was no longer weak and was able to stand unaided, diminutive and alone in the vast narthex of a mighty cathedral.

Then, as though dawn were breaking, a blade of light crept slowly to my feet. Warmth wrapped tenderly about me. Beyond was the arch of heaven, magnificent and immeasurable. From it, curtains of dazzling gold reached down to a flight of pure white steps. I waited in the blinding reflection of the drapes until they should open and let me in.

I tried to move forward. I wanted to run and mount those steps, but some unseen power held me back. 'Not yet. Your time has not yet come,' it seemed to say. Every fibre of my earthly being craved to be allowed to go forward. The curtains shimmered and began to open. Beyond, a dazzling eye of light prevented me from seeing more. The curtains closed, as though God had changed His mind, but His light was still with me. It seared my eyeballs and as I lifted my arm in protection, I hit something hard.

Opening my eyes, I found my hand had hit the locker. The morning sun streamed across my bed. The One Judge had decreed that my term in hell should be continued. Perhaps it would not be for long. I glanced at the humped figure of my companion and wondered what he had dreamed.

It was Wednesday, 23 October. I should be having a cake with forty-three candles on it. Instead, if my luck held, I would have rice! My thoughts were interrupted by the stamping of feet near the door. I noted the time was precisely seven o'clock. The five Japanese guards marched to my bed. The story I had heard, then, was true. We were to die, and I was to be the first to go.

Hall was staring as though he had seen a ghost; the guard commander, too, looked nonplussed. His men moved uneasily down the aisle. Now the reason for the hitch was plain. A solemn-faced nun stood just inside the door holding a tray. The Japs shuffled slowly away towards the verandah as if afraid of the regal figure. She was tall for a woman and wore the black habit and starched white wimple with grace. Her tray held two glasses and two bananas. She waited until the door had closed behind the Japanese, then seemed to glide into the space between our beds. Smiling, she placed a banana and a glass on either side of the locker top. I looked at the beautiful face and softly muttered my thanks. Then as gently as she had come, she left.

Jack reached for his banana with a baffled look on his face. I took up the fruit, skinned it, and began to eat. It had a vile taste. I retched, spat it out and reached for the glass. I had a quick drink of water from my glass and suddenly my lips were burning! Rubbing them with the corner of my sheet I knew the 'gift' had been doctored. Hall shouted that I had gone mad, but when I told him to eat my banana, he lamely stated that he had already eaten his, and turned his back on me.

Then I knew there was to be no execution. The whole diabolical scheme had been planned by Treverrow. The Japs were his friends, the types he could 'fix' things with. They had played their part well and had fooled me completely. The unpredictable Japanese, conquerors who collaborated with the vanquished. How correctly the police officer had assessed them, and Hall too, the British Judas and actor. But his final curtain would not be of gold like the one that hung before the gateway to heaven.

The stamp of the sadistic genius had been given when the woman appeared. She seemed genuine enough, so I could only guess she knew nothing of the 'doctoring' and had been persuaded by Treverrow to make the gift. He, I knew, was a member of the nun's church.

I had no illusions that my persecution was at an end but nothing Redbeard could devise would be as bad as the scheme last night. If only I had a friend to talk to, it would have made all the difference. Zainal's moral support, though helpful, was not sufficient.

The Black Marketeer was absent from the ward several times during the next two or three days, and one day before breakfast the doctor entered, and walking straight to Treverrow, told him to pack his things as he was returning to gaol immediately. Despite Redbeard's frenzied protestations, the doctor insisted he was fit to be discharged and left the ward.

The police superintendent and two constables arrived. The officer briskly ordered the Black Marketeer to pick up his bags, and when Grandos offered to carry one he was told to put it down. It was a pleasant sight to see Treverrow staggering under the weight of his ill-gotten gains while being hurried from the ward. The door closed behind him. I felt my spirits lift as though something evil had been purged from the ward.

By the last week of October, I was finally strong enough to stand for a length of time and the doctor declared I would be discharged as fit on November 2 and returned to gaol. I learned that two PoW camps were being erected at Sungei Ron, near Bukit Tinggi, one for military personnel, the other for civilians. Neither would be ready for occupation until late November, which meant waiting in gaol until I could be moved there. Hall and Good had already been sent back to gaol despite their protests.

Sungei Ron [Sungei Geron] camp began to loom as solid as the Twin Sisters mountains in Padang. I visualised rows of huts behind a wall of barbed wire. At least the clean wind could blow through that. In my mind I could see the tussocky grass slopes of the mountains, so reminiscent of the Lake District's Saddleback. I yearned for the sun and fresh air and to be among my own countrymen again, to rid myself of this fetid atmosphere that had sapped my starved, pale body. I wanted to see the moon and the stars instead of this dirty, white-panelled ceiling.

It was raining hard on the morning I was to be released but a cheerfulness possessed me. After nine weeks and three days of utter misery and longing, I was to take a full-blooded part in the business of being a prisoner of war.

The police van turned off the main road and rocked through deep puddles of water. Clambering out of the van I walked to a wicket gate and was led across a paved courtyard to the office. The police superintendent put out his hand and greeted me like an old friend instead of his latest gaolbird, then waved me to a chair and pushed over tobacco and papers, warning me to put it out if any Japs approached. He led me inside and introduced me to the number one prisoner in charge, explaining that pre-war he was the local bank manager, name of Gogh. The super assured me I would be in the British Military Camp inside a month.

A tall grey-haired man who would have looked more appropriate dressed in clerical attire than with a towel round his middle, solemnly approached us. The superintendent introduced him as Mynheer Wilhelm Gogh, responsible for the conduct of the prisoners in this section. Giving Gogh my name he asked that I be given bed space. Giving a short bow in acknowledgement of my existence, Gogh asked me to follow him. There was no friendliness in his tone or manner. Entering the room, we walked round the end of a large central wooden bench and down the other side.

Pointing to a couple of bare planks he indicated the uninviting space that was to be my bed. Gogh explained that Hall slept on one side with Good close by. One side was occupied by a George Schopmeyer. Gogh's manner had been curt to the point of downright rudeness. He had given no information as to where the latrines or the bathroom were or even the times that meals were issued and where.

My new neighbour George Schopmeyer, Netherlands Naval Air Service, was a tall, blond giant. I was pleased and surprised at his friendliness and the fact that he was in the military. He explained that his plane had been shot down by the Japs and he had been there only the last two days. I placed his age at twenty-eight and his height topping the six-foot mark. My new friend offered me a blanket to use on the hard planks. He reached for his plate and I realized it must be time for lunch. I went to Gogh who was sitting with two friends each of whom held plate and mug in readiness to join the queue for food. I asked for a plate and mug but was told I should have asked earlier as he hurried off to join the others.

Walking to the gate, I told the constable about my problem. He went away, then handed me the utensils with the superintendent's apology and added that he had been one of the men involved in my capture. Thanking him for his kindness, I joined the tail of the queue. On boxes outside the cookhouse, Good served the rice and Hall the coffee. I knew both had seen me but when it was my turn to be served, the *kuali* [cooking pot] was empty. The corporal looked up as if surprised there should be anyone else and, pretending not to know that I was in the gaol, called to his friend saying he was sorry that no food was left.

I returned to Gogh and asked him to arrange some rations for me. 'Mr Gogh,' I began, 'will you please instruct the cooks to issue me with a ration of rice?'

Before speaking, with exaggerated care he placed on his plate the leg of a chicken. He knew every eye was on him and considered his reply with a seriousness he might have used when intending to foreclose on a customer's security for defaulting on an overdraft. Then he looked up and said heavily, 'You should have got into the queue earlier. This kind of thing happens sometimes.'

As I accused him of being childish his face blanched with anger. Treverrow spoke rapidly to him in Dutch as I waited for an answer. Only Schopmeyer, my neighbour on the sleeping bench, smiled as if he were enjoying the showdown.

For the second time within ten minutes I walked to the gate. As I approached the watching constable, it struck me that perhaps Treverrow had omitted to tell Gogh that I spoke Malay and he now waited to enjoy the amusing spectacle of my miming my needs, under the impression that he would have to be called in to interpret. Then he could twist the conversation to suit himself.

Asking me what the fuss was about, the warder nodded his understanding as I launched a tirade against the chief prisoner. Gogh heard my invective and called out loudly that he would fix it. Then he came hurrying to me, but he was too late, his link with officialdom was lost.

'What's the trouble, Captain?' boomed the superintendent's voice. 'Is it true that you've had no food?' The keys dangled in the lock. As I explained to the superintendent what had happened, he looked angrily at Gogh and asked why there wasn't enough food for me. As the superintendent walked toward the cookhouse with Gogh meekly following, Hall appeared in the doorway carrying a piled-up plate of rice and behind him was a worried-looking corporal.

The superintendent roared at the men and threatened to put them in solitary if they continued this treatment. Thoroughly frightened, both nodded. Warning them not to put a foot wrong from now on, he ordered them to give me my rice. Judas Jack put it on my plate and the superintendent turned to Gogh ordering him to get someone else in the cookhouse, stating that if there was any more trouble he would stop private rations coming into the gaol.

I returned to my quarters to eat the rice, which was a much larger portion than I suspected was normal. Gogh found himself being blamed for having caused the contretemps, while he in turn accused Treverrow. Finally, the position of cook was filled by two dark-skinned Dutchmen and Gogh proceeded with his secretarial work.

My blond Dutch neighbour came up to me, making no attempt to conceal a broad grin. 'You've given me the first laugh I've had since coming in here.'

He was powerfully built and carried not an ounce of fat. He had grey eyes and his large nose was made more prominent by an ugly scar that stretched across it and halfway over his left cheek. It must have been quite a wound. He told me that Treverrow had prepared everyone for my arrival, as I had guessed.

On November 28, the superintendent informed us we were to be transferred to the military 'O' Camp (MULO), near Palembang. He then asked if there was anything he could get for us and said he would arrange to give us a towel and some other necessities. Wishing us the best of luck, he shook hands with me and then with George. As he turned to go, he said he hoped we would meet again in happier circumstances. The superintendent was big in more than stature. His kindness showed him to be a first-class human being by any standard.

Shortly a constable came in with a bundle under his arm. George opened it and to our great joy found not only a towel each but also toothbrushes and tubes of toothpaste. Could the police officer have known the thrill he gave us it would have been some small repayment for his kindness.

After breakfast on Saturday morning, a constable told us to get ready to move. The gate clanged behind us and through the bars I could see a face with a red beard looking through more bars at the further end of the yard.

## Chapter 10

# Palembang 'O' Camp, MULO

Outside the office, we met the superintendent and the Japanese sergeant who had originally captured Hall and me. The latter eyed us up and down as though we were a load of pigs about to be taken to the slaughterhouse. We were made to unroll our luggage. After the inspection, he '*ushed*' us through the wicket gate to a canvas-covered van, like the one that had brought me from the hospital. George and I took the port seat and Hall and Good the other. The driver was a civilian Indonesian wearing a Jap-type cap and a brassard on his arm showing he had been pressed into service with the Japanese Imperial Army.

We travelled until the sun had set and I was almost frozen when my Dutch friend pointed to some newly constructed sheds with *attap* roofs and walls. The fence surrounding them was about fifty yards back from the road. Each building was 150 feet in length and 20 feet in width. It was obviously a camp and covered many acres.

The Jap made no attempt to slow down. Then we saw a large party of men marching out of one of the two gates that were divided by a forty-foot gap wired on either side. Quite plainly there were two camps. The men turned in the direction in which we were travelling and both George and I broke into a smile as we heard the strains of 'Waltzing Matilda'.

We realised they were 'our boys' and must be a working party. George was suggesting that the two camps were for civilian men and women, when more huts appeared.

The driver turned in at a gateway flanked by two towering posts and came to a stop opposite what was obviously a guardroom. Telling us to get down, the driver handed us over to the sergeant of the guard, who with a brusque '*Ush!*' drove us into a small office. A European, dressed in khaki shorts and a well-patched shirt and wearing a British naval officer's cap, followed us in. He introduced himself as Lieutenant Lyle.

At the door we met a heavy, moustached man, looking odd in shorts made from a piece of tartan-printed cotton material. He was of medium height and almost bald. Bushy eyebrows protected his fierce, dark eyes and the grip of his hand as he welcomed me was equally fierce. This was Colonel Hill.

The two other ranks were handed over to the sergeant major for allotment of accommodation, while Schopmeyer and I were taken to a hut in the officers' lines and given bed spaces. The hut had been sectioned crosswise. We had no sooner introduced ourselves than supper was served from a four-gallon petrol tin. It was a lucky day for us newcomers and as we sat at the plank table on a plank form I said how pleased I was to be eating meat with my rice. This remark went down as a classic and was ever after held against me. Nevertheless, I was allowed to finish the meal before a big black snail was placed on my bed amid much laughter.

Men of the three fighting services were our companions. They hailed from Britain, Australia and New Zealand and of course Holland was represented by George Schopmeyer, my friend and neighbour. On the bamboo slats at my other side was an Ordnance Corps officer named Bramble, popularly called Bram, who gave us some 'gen'. A senior officer had charge of each hut section and was responsible for his men appearing on parade for *tenko* [roll call], which took place morning and evening under Jap supervision. The Japs were so scared of air raids that the use of matches or lighters outside was prohibited and no lights were allowed even in the huts.

The moon was up and Bram took us to the *benjo* [toilet], some distance over the crest of a rise and near the perimeter wire. Bramble explained that the place had been chopped up into separate compartments and floored with planks, asking us to please remember to close the lid because the flies were something chronic!

As George was wondering how you could find your way over there on a dark night, Bramble told him to catch fireflies and put them in a little bag of mosquito netting, saying they gave out a helluva good glow. Seeing our sceptical faces, he assured us he would demonstrate once back in the hut. Our guide was as good as his word and we were astounded at the light given by the phosphorescent insects. After this demonstration, we were prepared to believe almost anything, and we showed no surprise when he told us that everyone smoked a compound of cured papaya and cherry leaves.

We had dropped into a world where ingenuity counted much more than wealth. Finding the most comfortable position on my bed, I lay listening to the quiet hum of talk against the background of chirruping cicadas, hoping to be able to contribute my full share to this unorthodox way of living.

We were fast asleep when Bramble drawled, '*Tenko* in five minutes, chaps,' and looking at my watch, I shuddered. It was only three o'clock!

Commander Moorhead told me that the Japs worked on Tokyo time and I had better advance my watch by two hours! A blast from a whistle shot us out of bed and we lined up with the others outside the hut and went through the farce of dressing ranks though the only man who could see the markers was the one next to him. In the distance I could hear the troops marking off on their parade ground, then all was quiet.

At the sound of approaching footsteps, the colonel called us to attention. The Jap ordered us to number and, like a machine gun cracking, high-pitched voices followed low ones down the front rank. Several times this was repeated, each faster than before and I realised that this was a game to baffle the guard commander. In a loud whisper the colonel gave him the total number of officers on parade, and in return the Jap allowed us to be '*ushed*'. Moments later everyone returned to the huts. 'One *tenko* less,' was the general cry.

After breakfast Bram took us on a tour of the camp. I estimated its area as between forty and fifty acres. Learning there were 3,000 prisoners, I did a bit of rapid town planning to find we lived at a density of sixty persons to the acre, much more liberal than I had expected.

We saw the miserable little hut our doctor used for a sick bay, the gardens, cookhouses and pig farm. A Nip was strolling near the piggery, causing Bramble to veer away. A sow was about to give birth and the man was there to count the piglets when they arrived, effectively scotching any attempt to relieve her of a couple of her offspring.

No sooner had we returned to the hut than George and I were required to attend the office, the last room of the hut on the corner of the parade ground. As we entered, the colonel told us to 'take a pew' and asked if either of us sang.

George laughed and said he had been thrown out of a choir while I assured him I only sang in the shower. The colonel told us he was trying to get a choir going and invited us to service at eleven o'clock on Sunday. This was followed by our telling him how we came to be captured, as he was gathering information about everyone's situation.

An hour elapsed before we left him. He sympathised with me about my wife being missing and promised to give me news when the women's camp was occupied. He warned us that all produce from the gardens or pig farm was for the exclusive use of the Japs and if caught, the Jap OC, Takahashi, believed in collective punishment. The colonel left us in no doubt that

Takahashi was a first-class bastard. He went on to say that George would have to go out on working parties and that light work would be found for me until I was strong enough to earn heavy rations. Seeing a questioning look on my face, he explained that the Japs issued rations at the rate of 150 grams of rice per day to heavy workers, just over five ounces for three meals. Light-duty workers got 100 grams and the sick, nothing at all. The latter had, therefore, to be fed from the rations of the workers. Even these figures must be cut by twenty-five per cent for the weight of stones, wood and pieces of coal that had to be sifted from the bagged rice sweepings.

Bramble met us on the way back asking with a grin if the 'Poona Panther' had tried to get us to join his choir. We said he had but got no takers. It turned out that the colonel was the padre and was always encouraging the men to attend his services. Bram told us that some of them went to support the old full-o'-guts Panther and that he sometimes was able to give them the latest news that Chisholm passed on. He paused and said he shouldn't have mentioned his name as hiding a radio was a quick way to die if found out. It turned out that before the war Chisholm was an announcer for the Aussie Broadcasting Corporation and now, while in the cookhouse every night, he went out through the wire to the set. A patrolling Jap had only to hear him sneeze or crack a twig and he was a goner.

When attending our first 'service' Bram pointed out Chisholm as he came towards the hut. I saw a man above average height and very thin, even by PoW standards. A mop of close-cropped brown hair crowned a long, lantern-jawed face. His lips were compressed into a straight line below a narrow aquiline nose. But it was the man's eyes that held my attention. They were grey and as cold as a piece of ice.

At the further side of the human circle stood Hall and Good and behind them a smiling Sergeant Major MacLaren who had roped them into his party. They both avoided looking in our direction. For a time one of the guards hung around but cleared off as we sang the repetitive verses. The service ended with 'God Save the King'. The Panther looked in all directions to make sure the Jap had gone, then, apparently concluding his devotions, he almost intoned the news that the tide of war had turned. We had won the battle of El Alamein. Rommel's forces had been completely routed. He added, 'You can pass the word round quietly but no high jinks, remember, or the Japs might smell a rat.'

Delighted with the news, I looked at the man who had risked his life to get it for us, and saw him turn towards the cookhouse, poker-faced and taciturn as though he knew nothing of the glad tidings.

Suddenly a rumpus sounded from the direction of the men's quarters and George went outside to see what it was all about. A Jap was beating up Hall. The sergeant major stood near trying to intervene but the guard would have none of it. The colonel came hurrying from his hut and demanded to know why one of his men was being beaten up. The Jap held up a piece of wood and for a moment I thought he was going to hit the Panther, but instead he brought it down on Hall's head with a thwack that made us shiver. The man collapsed in a heap and would have been hit again had not the colonel stepped in front of the guard. Foiled in his attempt, the madman threw the wood away and flat-handed the CO. Then after haranguing him, the Jap walked away. Some of the troops carried the unconscious man into his hut as the angry colonel called for the doctor.

Later we learned from the sergeant major that Hall, when passing the men's cookhouse, picked up a piece of firewood and, being elated by the news, threw it high in the air, yelling, 'Alamein's bust!' The log came down near the Jap who alleged it had been thrown at him. The incident, we were informed, had certainly ended the announcement of news at church services.

On my circuit of the camp I noticed that all carrying was done by a couple of men with a pole on their shoulders and a four-gallon petrol tin slung between them. I had also seen some discarded planks near the *benjo*, and gathering these together in the shade of a tree, went hunting for a saw.

Two days later and not withstanding its Heath Robinson appearance, the camp's first wheelbarrow went into service. The Japanese soon recognised the value of such transport for work in the garden and at the pig farm. In January 1943 I was placed in charge of the camp workshops. I was given more planks and ordered to go into production, but I stalled, saying that my friends had helped me to make the first one by forming nails from old scraps of wire. If they expected good service from the barrows, they would have to be better constructed. This could only be done if we had the proper tools. Imoyotu, the second in command, considered my request to be reasonable and before the week was out we had chisels, nails and another saw. Bram and George too were seconded for the work but my greatest pleasure was that the Japs reckoned wheelbarrow-making qualified me for heavy rations. I would no longer have to exist partly on the sweat of others.

Inside a month, a small fleet was being trundled about the camp and their usefulness made everyone wonder how the place had ever run without them. We had entered our new life with a practical contribution.

From such lowly beginnings, a workshop was started, and a small building erected on the site of our original activities. Word was passed to the troops who went out on working parties, asking them to bring back anything that might be useful. Day after day materials flowed in: bits of chain, wire, solder, small bottles of spirits of salts, glass and nails. The men vied with each other and it was amazing to see the variety and size of the things they produced from their G-strings. Or if a decent guard happened to be in charge of the party, bars of steel, sheets of old corrugated iron, timber and sometimes pieces of Perspex were carried in. The stores and airfield parties were the chief sources of supply and the items enabled us to make scalpels, a man-sized weighing machine, a still for the manufacture of surgical spirit and a hundred-and-one things such a community needed, even to sundials.

Many of the sick owed their lives to this organised system of thieving, because until it started, the doctor could do nothing more than give advice. The exasperated medico, for all his pleading with Lieutenant Nakai the Japanese medical officer, and the many promises made, received not a square inch of bandage, let alone any surgical instruments. Even open wounds had to be bound with the remnants of someone's shirt. Therefore when prisoners were required to unload medical stores from train or lorry, they stole medicines at random and at great risk, not knowing what they had pilfered until the labels had been deciphered by the two officers who could read the script. Medicines were given to the doctor and materials to the workshop. Some paid the supreme penalty for trying to help their prisoner comrades and others were maimed for life, but the game went on as it had to if we were to survive.

One morning the doctor came to the workshop and asked if I could make a special type of bed for a man who had dysentery and was not improving because he had to be moved so often to use the commode. I agreed to try.

Two days later the bed was finished. It had a moveable middle section that gave access to a pan supported on runners. A sectional mattress, a rice sack stuffed with grass, caused it to be named our *deluxe* model. It was with something approaching pride that we carried the bed to the sick bay and demonstrated the technical details. The patient was fetched, and I looked into the close-set eyes of Hall as he was laid gently on the only mattress and the only single bed in camp, a piece of furniture designed by the man he had termed a bastard. Without a word, George walked outside. Bram and I followed.

It was reported that the civilian camps were being occupied. Colonel Hill, in accordance with his promise, gave me permission to take charge of the airport working party on the morrow. Borrowing shorts and boots for the occasion, I almost danced my way into the workshop to give my friends the good news. I would have to pass the camps and it was possible my wife would see me, even if I could not pick her out from the many women who would be watching us through the wire fence. She might not be there of course, but I was determined to find out.

The sun cast long shadows as we closed the shop door and Bram whispered, 'Red light,' which was the universal signal that a Jap was in camp. A Jap was pinning something on the noticeboard. We walked over to see a notice that said all commands from tomorrow were to be given in Japanese! There followed a list of some sixty orders.

My first time out and I had to deal with this! A noise from the men's parade ground and a crowd around their notice board showed that a similar notice had been posted for the NCOs to digest.

I wouldn't have minded if they had posted the list in the morning or even an hour before, but it would be dark in twenty minutes and dark when I left in the morning, leaving me no chance of a refresher. Seemed I'd be in for a beating because I knew I wouldn't be able to remember those tongue-twisters.

For as long as the light lasted and with others breathing down my neck I concentrated on learning the Japanese for 'Eyes left', etc., but the only command I had no difficulty in remembering was the most stupid and unlikely one, '*Fuzi*' [lie down]. Who the hell wanted to do that? If bombs started to fall they would be our bombs and we would be jumping about for joy.

Next morning I heard the sergeant major's Cockney voice ringing across the camp marshalling the men for the party. Dawn was breaking as we marched off the parade ground, MacLaren in the rear with me. The guard would be picked up by the gate. So far all the orders had been given quietly in English, but as we approached the guardroom where the Jap on duty generally sat in a big armchair on a raised dais, I concentrated on the Japanese words for 'Eyes left'. I yelled '*Kashirah hidari*,' hoping I had remembered correctly. Every head turned dutifully to the left and I was pleased to see the 'chairman' stand and return the salute with a bow. So far so good but I was worried about the command for 'Eyes front'. I racked my mind for the Japanese order. In a flap, I turned to the sergeant major and asked him, 'What's "Eyes front"?'

No sooner were the words out of my mouth than he roared, 'Ripe Strawberry!' Every head was turned smartly to the front as we passed through the gateway. The first obstacle had been overcome and the quick-witted Cockney had earned himself a title.

As we reached the women's camp high-pitched female cheers and hand-waving greeted us. I searched among the faces for my beloved wife. The faces of the women appeared like a wavy chalk line, featureless except where capped with black or silver hair. I tried to blame emotion for my blurred vision, but I realised the truth with a shock. My eyes were not as good as they had been and would most probably become worse on the starvation diet. We passed the forty-foot gap and came to the civilian men's camp. I felt a little cheered about my eyes when I had no difficulty picking out Treverrow's flaming red beard next to the giant Grandos.

Two miles further on we came to a small *kampong* [village] and fifty yards beyond turned into a lane leading to the airfield. Given the task of lengthening the airstrip, the guard demanded a cubic metre of the hard, compacted laterite earth be moved by each man under the pain of feeling his stick across their shoulders. At the end of the day *chungkals* [shovels] and spades were stacked in readiness for the following day's party and we marched back.

Dusk was gathering as we again passed the internees' camps. The tired troops whistled as cheerily as they had done in the morning. Treverrow and his friend might never have moved, for they stood in the same place alongside a mob of sullen, staring men. Their attitude seemed the stranger by contrast with the cheering women.

'*Kashirah*' and a growl got us safely past the guardroom. When we had been dismissed, I reported to the colonel on the working party, giving him our nickname for the guard on duty, any beatings he had performed, and the type of work done. He asked me whether I had seen my wife and I had to admit failure.

Bramble and George wanted to know how I had got on with giving Japanese orders and I retailed the story of 'Ripe Strawberry' amid much laughter. They were disappointed for me that I had not been able to pick out my wife and wished me better luck next time.

The following morning, I was back in the workshop and had just finished riveting a set of broken dentures when a Korean guard known as Tor walked in. He was a big man, and although he professed to be a Christian, had given almost as many beatings as the most detested guard, Leggings. Now he stuck his British-made rifle under my nose and demanded I make a new piling swivel to replace the one he had broken. I pointed out it was a difficult job but said I would try, telling him to come back at two o'clock. Reluctantly leaving the weapon, he went back to the supervision of the garden fatigue.

Luckily, we had a length of eight-inch copper wire. Cleaning a piece of it with sand, I snipped it off, fitted it through the holes of the saddle and bent it to the correct shape. As far as the instructions went, the job was done. Then we did a little work of our own by tapping the foresight out of line. George suggested we open up the magazine spring, making it too stiff to put any rounds in. I thought it was good idea until Bram took out the bolt and started filing the firing pin.

He suggested this was much more 'to the point', grinning at his own joke. As he filed, the Dutchman sat in the doorway cleaning the weapon while I drained the oil bottle for our own use. When the work was done, I doubted the rifle had ever been cleaned so thoroughly. And it would not be our fault if Tor got the 'stick' at his next guard parade.

We were not surprised to see the distrustful guard coming to the shop fully an hour before the appointed time. Bram, who in the Service was an ordnance officer, picked up the rifle and was giving it a final polish when the door was unceremoniously kicked open. Tor's glowering expression changed into a beaming smile as he looked at the gleaming weapon and, inspecting the swivel, announced that we had done a good job. It was a good thing he did not know how good!

Tor threw a packet of cigarettes on the bench and wiped his hands on the seat of his pants, afraid of dirtying the rifle. Then with a nod of appreciation he left, gloating over the useless thing he carried. Work was suspended while the staff each enjoyed a whole cigarette and agreed that not even the colonel should be told of the incident. If the Japs should find out we would be eliminated but we were prepared to take that risk. The real danger lay in Tor being sent on a firing course.

Like guilty conspirators, we jumped at the sound of footsteps and pretended to be busy when a timid 'Excuse me, sir' made the three of us look round. It was Good. Self-consciously, with his hand before his mouth, he asked if we had finished his teeth. Without a word I handed them to him and a moment later the domino dentures appeared as of old.

In the afternoon, Gladys, the bespectacled guard commander, arrived with Tor and ordered me to replace *his* piling swivel with a shiny one like Tor's. Cautiously I pretended to object. There was nothing wrong with the original swivel and Lieutenant Takahashi, the officer in charge of the camp, might blame me for damaging the rifle. We would clean it for him if that was what he wanted. He tapped the copper swivel of Tor's rifle and put two packets of cigarettes on the bench to convince me. I accepted the task and asked him to leave his rifle for an hour. Pointing to the time on his watch he went out smiling and George took up his sentry duty at the door.

A new swivel was made while Bram filed the striker pin. For the second time that day we denuded a rifle of oil and polished it to a degree that would have won praise from Sergeant Major MacLaren himself. When Gladys returned, he was so delighted with the result that he added another packet of cigarettes to his payment and went back to the guardroom with the dud *bundook* [rifle].

It had been a great day. But it became even greater when I learned from Norry Cook, an officer who had been in the hospital at Bukit Tinggi, that my wife had also been a patient and had just returned to camp in the lorry with him. He handed me a letter from her, written just in case a Captain Jennings happened to be a fellow prisoner. Not daring to be seen with anything that looked like a letter, I put it in my pocket and asked Cook if there was any possibility of getting one back to her. He said it was possible, and said to ask anyone being sent for operations or teeth extractions to hand it to the matron for forwarding. Evidently there were plenty passing between the internee men and their wives. Norry was booked for another check-up next week, so could take one for me.

I thanked him and hurried away to the *benjo* to read and re-read my wife's letter, which told me she was fit and well after having had a 'touch' of dysentery. I knew she had tried to minimise her illness and put me at ease should I ever get the message. To know that she was alive and only a few hundred yards from me made my heart bound with joy. After memorising every word, I destroyed the precious note.

The colonel seemed to be almost as pleased as I was when he knew I had word from my wife. He suggested I take a day off from the workshop and use his office to write my reply, where there were not only pencil and paper but a runner-guard on duty to warn me in case of intrusion by the Japs.

The following day I wrote my letter and sealed it with a dab of latex. I addressed it to 'Midge', my pet name for my wife, in case anything should go wrong and the letter fall into Jap hands. The addressee would be untraceable, and persecution avoided. All such letters would go to the lady commandant, and even if my wife did not call at her office, the word would go around that a letter awaited someone named Midge. She would immediately know it was from me. The 'service' to Bukit Tinggi was erratic but the doctor informed me he had a lorry going there with a hernia case next day and he would give the letter to the orderly.

With a feeling of greater happiness and contentment than for many a long day, I walked across to the workshop in time to see another guard leaving with a shining piling swivel. My friends greeted me with a cigarette and told me he was the second that morning. Tor had certainly started a fashion in copper piling swivels and more wire was urgently needed if the good work was to be kept up. Two more guards were similarly obliged during the afternoon and an SOS for large-gauge copper wire was sent over to the men who would be going out on working parties the next day.

In the next three weeks, I went out of camp several times and each time searched the faces of the women for the one I most wanted to see. Cook and others had taken letters for me to Bukit Tinggi, but so far I had received no reply to the first one I had written and I was beginning to get worried. The one I had given to Norry had contained thirty guilders from the raffling of my watch and ring.

At last an answer came to two of my letters and I could have jumped with joy when I learned the cash had arrived safely. She'd had to sell her engagement ring but that was of no account. When we got out of this mess, I would buy her another with diamonds as big as walnuts if she wanted it. Just looking at her squiggly writing filled me with a happiness that hurt, particularly as I knew the note must be destroyed.

The brave tone of her letter put new life into me. She mentioned having the job of hut captain and that meant being responsible for the conduct of the women in her hut, an unpleasant task. There was also a piano, which she was doing her best to tune with a pair of pliers to have it ready for the concert they intended holding at Christmas, only a month away. The women were engaged in making toys for the many children who were in the camp and she suggested we make some too and ask the Japanese for permission to send them.

Colonel Hill spoke to both officers and men about the matter and in a short time wooden dolls with sacking hair and small nut bracelets began to make their appearance, together with railway engines, swings and a variety of other toys. About this time we had a visit from a Jap colonel, and the Panther was fortunate enough to obtain his permission to send them. Striking while the iron was hot, we bagged the lot then and there for transmission by the Jap ration lorry.

After Christmas I received my next letter and it conveyed the thanks of all the mothers and those looking after children whose mothers had died for the wonderful toys we had sent. I read that part of my wife's letter to the colonel, and in his own inimitable fashion he expressed the women's gratitude to all troops on parade.

My wife said she had seen me with a working party on two occasions, and I resolved to get detailed for one as often as possible. Before I could do anything about it, however, the balloon went up and the hospital at Bukit Tinggi was closed all in one day. Women and troops who had been operated on the previous day were sent back to camp, and one of our men still under anaesthetic was taken from the table with the operation only half done. The Dutch doctor who had performed miracles of surgery was taken into the hospital grounds and shot out of hand. All this happened through the carelessness of a woman returning to camp. Not expecting her suitcase to be searched, she had put all the letters inside the suitcase on top of her clothes without any attempt at hiding them. When the Jap lifted the lid on his perfunctory inspection, a dozen or more of them lay facing him. The matron and nurses were badly beaten up and sent into camp. Then a few days later another blow fell. The women were sent away, we knew not where, and their camp was deserted. My anxiety about my wife was renewed.

I abandoned my endeavours to be sent out on working parties and turned my attention to increasing the size of the sick bay to hospital proportions and, of necessity, the mortuary as well.

# Chapter 11

# Hero for a Day

George prepared the *attap* while Bramble and I erected the framework of a new ward, to the great delight of our harassed doctor, Surgeon-Lieutenant Patrick Corcoran, RN. Officially, Paddy was supposed to live in our hut but since the closing down of the hospital at Bukit Tinggi the demand on his services had been so great that we had built a bunk for him in the operating theatre where he could take catnaps and be on call at all times.

One morning he asked if we could convert the dysentery bed into one suitable for a man with a compound leg fracture. He used up most of the earth floor with screwdriver drawings and explained that some system of adjustment for leg height would be necessary.

We got to work and fixed corner posts to the bed with a stiffening rail round the top to carry the transom bar. Bramble hit on the happy idea of boring holes in the uprights like the legs of an easel and fitting them with captive pegs. Paddy was delighted with the result and installed his patient in the unfinished wing where he could watch us and 'keep his mind off his leg'.

Resuming our work on the building we were surprised to see a dozen Sikhs being taken on a conducted tour of the camp. When they arrived at the hospital we saw they all wore Jap emblems on their chests and were speaking Nippon Go. Later that day a bigger surprise awaited us when we found they had taken over the internal duties of the camp from the Koreans. This was just another little lesson in humiliation. Still, two could play that game and the Indians suffered considerable embarrassment from 'old sweats' who'd had service in India and who told them in their own dialect what they thought of their defection. These Japanese puppets retaliated by reporting mythical incidents which caused the Japs to make raids night after night, during which we had to stand on the parade ground until every hut had been searched. This treatment had repercussions on working parties, as men who had stood half the night were physically incapable of completing any work and as a result were beaten up.

Dawn broke in all its glory as we arrived at the hospital. After a couple of abortive attempts to climb to the uncovered rafters, Bramble and George managed it with the aid of a few earthy expressions and painful grimaces. I threw them a bunch of rattan lashings and several pieces of *attap* and was about to go inside to tie the rattan knots when I heard the angry voice of Leggings. Peering round the corner of the building I saw the vile little guard leaning on his stick. By his side was Ringer, who acted as interpreter, and in front of them the doctor, who had obviously been examining the long queue of outpatients. Leggings wanted to know why the work parties were below strength and so many men sick. Paddy replied he should look at the boys' feet as it was obvious they couldn't walk ten yards.

Ringer pointed to the men's feet and gave the unnecessary explanation. But the yellow wretch had only the basest of primeval instincts in his chemical composition. He struck the doctor, then started laying about among the men, leaving some in such a state that they would never work again, even if they managed to get back home. Only the thought of Jasper Dunbar's torture and death at the hands of the *Kempeitai* for punching a guard unconscious in retaliation for unjust punishment kept the doctor from strangling the swine then and there. Leggings sensed he had done enough damage and turned away, leaving comrades helping comrades and the doctor helping everybody.

On his way back to the parade ground, the guard ran straight into the men who were doing the heavy job of water carrying. Without any thought for the 3,000 prisoners whose rice could neither be washed nor boiled in the absence of this vital commodity, he commandeered the whole sixteen and ordered them to the working party.

Before Leggings could get out of camp, however, the colonel remonstrated with the guard commander who finally agreed to allow us to retain two of the men for the essential water chore. Others would have to be impressed if anyone were to have any food. The workshop staff volunteered to assist but the doctor pointed out there were others not engaged in such important work as we were, and that completion of the extension was imperative. So we got on with the job of roofing and occasionally passed a cheery word to the fractured-leg patient, whom Bram persisted in calling 'Jessie' as his name happened to be Matthews [Jessie Matthews was an English actress].

Without warning, the Japanese doctor, Ishimario, and Takahashi walked in followed by the colonel and the interpreter, Ringer, and stopped at the foot of the bed. The Irishman bowed, turned and took a thermometer from the patient's mouth and read it with a nonchalance that seemed to annoy

Ishimario, who snapped at him. Ringer glumly translated the query as to why so many men were sick.

Paddy told the colonel that it was the marching and that he needed medicines and bandages to cure them more quickly. Paddy watched for the reaction on the Jap's face as his reply was being interpreted.

'He says they have none for themselves, but you've got to get these men out of here and build up their working strength. He also wants to know what this case is.'

'Tell the silly divil he's got the toothache!' was Paddy's curt reply.

Though the interpreter replied to the Jap, we all knew that he did not tell the man what Paddy had said. The red weal across Ringer's face was sufficient indication that he had already said something that had not pleased someone that morning.

Gripping his sword as some Victorian lady might have lifted her dress when stepping into her carriage, Ishimario, with a smile at his companion, walked round the bed. The colonel watched him with a face as black as a thundercloud. The man in the shining jackboots stopped to sneer at the contraption for adjustment of which we were so proud. The pan of stones that provided the counterweight also came in for his contempt. Then smiling superciliously, he took a silk handkerchief from his pocket and, holding it to his thick nose, inspected the rag-bound splintered limb.

From red-rimmed eyes Jessie stared at the man who had it in his power to help him. The frail, fleshless figure, naked except for his G-string and the rags about his broken leg, lifted a drumstick arm in mute appeal. Ishimario smiled into the face with the sunken cheeks and brought his gaze slowly down the body to the deep shadows where the collarbones protruded, then to the ribs and indented stomach. Finally, as if he had come to a conclusion, he again smiled at Takahashi and, replacing his handkerchief, turned to the sick man. With one swipe of his hand he knocked the pegs out and the injured leg fell with a crash across the other. There was a horrible, piercing scream.

As Paddy rushed to his patient I saw the colonel's knuckles whiten. Takahashi's hand closed round the hilt of his sword and the old man made no further move. Nothing could be done to help Jessie now if the look on the Irishman's face and the tender way in which he placed the man's arm by his side were anything to go by. Paddy Corcoran straightened up and glared his hate at the killer who called himself a doctor.

We had watched the whole affair through a gap in the *attap* wall. Now Bram tugged at my arm to urge me away so we couldn't be caught as witnesses to the murder. We hoped we would live long enough to see those two officers pay the penalty for what they had done that day. We were grateful the colonel hadn't done anything foolish as no doubt he would have been executed.

Bram and Schopmeyer went to get a box for 'Jessie' and I gathered banana leaves from the garden. Ten minutes later I returned and, lining the poor coffin with the leaves, the three of us started back for the hospital.

I heard my name called, and looking round saw the CO beckoning me. With him were the two Jap officers and the interpreter. I hurried over to find out what the old man wanted. He told me Lieutenant Takahashi wanted me to dig a well here as the water fatigue was to be discontinued. The work had to be done by men on their day off and Takahashi was to supervise the job himself. According to him there was plenty of water at this spot. The colonel asked me to do my best.

At parade time I told the troops of Takahashi's order about digging a well and of his intention to supervise the work himself; that if we got on with the work right away he might not interfere too much but the water fatigue was to be abolished as a permanent party.

At the spot indicated by Takahashi we scribed a circle twelve feet in diameter on the sun-baked earth and officers and men both began the compulsory task. Guards turned up to watch the unusual activity but made no attempt to interfere. Soil was dragged back from the lip of the hole and soon there was a sizeable mound. The work was proceeding admirably when the volunteer water fatigue came by. Suddenly a voice piped up, 'Oh my! A bunch of bloody prospectors!' Every man stopped digging and turned to see who had spoken. The Australian's quip had been directed at his best mate 'Ripe Strawberry' who threatened to get him to 'dig his way home!'

Sweat-caked dust covered everyone and after half an hour I called a halt for a smoko as there was a limit to what one could do in the hard red laterite and in the blazing sun. Cigarettes were rolled and sparks flew from tinderboxes as men enjoyed their *yasumi* [break]. Bramble and I sat on a heap of muck passing uncomplimentary remarks about George, whom we had left in the cool workshop to finish a job.

At that moment, Buck, serious-faced and staring, walked towards us holding a piece of wire between his hands. There were some comments about his sanity but still the Queenslander did not smile as he walked past us.

I got up to find out what the man was up to but MacLaren had beaten me to it and was striding after the retreating figure. When I got up to them Buck was telling the SM that we were wasting our time digging for water there. Asking him why he thought that, he told us he had put down a lot of bores in his time and that there was water where we now stood.

He held up the piece of wire, and handing it to me, showed me how to grip the two ends in both hands, explaining that if I had the right electricity in me, I would soon see what happened. As I walked off, he said he would start digging himself to show them how serious he was.

Holding the wire loop up as Buck had shown me, I gripped the ends hard and walked past the scoffers towards the diviner and the SM. Steadily I approached them and felt the wire trying to twist in my hands. Do what I might, the loop turned slowly to the earth until, at the spot where they were standing, the metal wrenched itself downwards and pointed to my feet. I was glad to let go the wire and rub my hands to ease the pain where it had dug into my flesh.

Buck smiled and assured me I had the 'electricity'. Evidently not everyone could water divine and Buck was glad I did, as I had proved his point. I was convinced and told Mac to shift location, no matter what Takahashi said.

The diviner and Mac each picked up a *chungkal* and began digging.

It was too much for Bramble. The circle within which to dig had not been scribed and his engineering soul could not tolerate such lack of precision. Grabbing the two pegs fastened to the rattan string, he hurried to Buck and, consulting him, banged in the centre peg and drew the circle.

Laughs mingled with grumbles. Queenslander and Cockney, rhythmically wielding their *chungkals*, were augmented by Bramble as he also started digging.

Mounds of loose earth grew to such proportions they had to be scattered over the surrounding area. Everyone seemed determined to reach the depth that had been reached in the dud well before the light failed.

My attention was distracted by shouting from the direction of the guardroom. Leggings' party had returned, and the little squirt was roaring his head off. Someone must have been found with something he ought not to have and, as usual, everyone had to pay the penalty.

Bram and I walked round the back of the cookhouse to try to find out what the trouble was. It had been a lousy day. First Jessie's death, then the dud well and now this, whatever it was. Peering around the corner of the building we were in time to see the guard put all his weight behind a stinging, flat-handed blow that landed on the face of a man even smaller than himself. It was Jock Muir, a Glaswegian and as tough as they come. With obvious delight that he could reach the man's face, Leggings gave him another broadside on the other cheek, then stopped in front of the next man to repeat the operation. But Corporal Storey was a tall man and the guard would have some difficulty in reaching his face. So he lifted his rifle and Storey tensed to receive the blow. Then something that had never happened before streaked like a comet through Leggings' firmament. Muir broke ranks and, yanking the guard's arm, pointed to his reddened face.

'Come on, *kasi lagi* [give me more].'

Leggings was not the only one who gasped at the man's audacity in asking for more. He laid his rifle down and advancing towards his victim with an evil leer, lashed out at him viciously. Both arms flailing, he struck his stupid enemy as if he were threshing a sheaf of corn. Legs apart, Muir balanced like a ballet dancer on his points, his face moving first to one side and then the other. Buck cringed and was wondering why on earth Muir had asked for more.

I explained that he and Storey were buddies and Leggings was going to ram the rifle butt into Storey's crotch. Jack was taking the comeback for it, but I wondered if he was beginning to regret it.

The guard finished and picked up his rifle. Muir's face was purple. The whole of the guard had by this time turned out and stood grinning as much at their compatriot as at the man foolish enough to ask for more. Now, for the second time, Leggings stepped in front of Storey. He looked tired but tried to brace himself, then turned with a grin to see if Muir would ask for more punishment. The Scot broke ranks again, turning the guard's grin into an incredulous snarl.

'Come on, you lousy yellow bastard! *Kasi lagi!*' And as though to make his persecutor even angrier, Muir laughed in his face.

Leggings again lay his rifle down. The assembled guard began to laugh out loud. This was first-class entertainment, the kind that Japs liked, where the advantage was all on their side. The arrogant prisoner had been lucky so far but soon he would be crying 'enough'.

The colonel came hurrying down the road to try to stop the one-sided affair, but the enraged guard had already begun his attack and was beating the daylights out of the Glaswegian. 'It's OK, sir,' the victim called out.

Taking this as an appeal for mercy, Leggings drew back, lowered his head between his shoulders, and in an effort to inflict the coup de grâce, catapulted himself like a battering ram at the man's stomach. Without moving his feet, Muir turned his body. Two men in the ranks behind him were bowled over as the human projectile, having missed its mark, shot between them and went slithering in the dust.

The other guards laughed uproariously, then scowled as the prisoners joined in. But the Scot started them laughing again by picking Leggings up out of the dust and setting him on his feet.

The sun had disappeared over the horizon, its lingering rays reflected from the clouds like an unseen torch. Unsteady and dishevelled, the persecutor leaned heavily on his victim's arm, unaware for the moment that he did so, but as the laughter of his comrades filtered into his consciousness, he shook himself free and walked out through the gate. Every eye fixed on the little wretch, who was suffering from loss of face more than anything else as he crossed the road to his own quarters.

The guard commander finished Leggings' work for him by dismissing the parade. Jock Muir had not only saved his friend from a beating but the rest of the party too, and he became the hero of the camp.

Incidents, most of them gruesome, had often happened before, giving everyone plenty to talk about. This time it was different. Through the courage of Muir, we had come out on top. From every hut came the strains of 'I belong tae Glesgy'.

The following day Muir was detailed for work at the well. Though his friends still applauded him, the taciturn man made no reply other than to smile and carry on with the digging. At half past ten, the message 'Red light' flashed round the camp. We worked on, keeping our eyes open to see who the Jap could be. Dixon spotted him first.

It was Leggings and Ringer was with him. As I pretended to be busy giving orders, our interpreter called out, 'Hello Mick, is Muir with you? This rat-bag wants a word with him.'

I called 'Jock!' down the hole. As Muir landed alongside me, begrimed and sweating, the guard came up all smiles and affability. He started speaking quickly and everybody waited with burning curiosity to know what it was all about.

'He says he is sorry he had to beat you yesterday because you are a very brave man.'

'Bullshit!' the Scotsman replied truculently.

'Further,' Ringer continued with a grin, 'he says as you kept on asking for more, he's brought you more and he expects that'll wipe the slate clean. Anyhow, don't be an idiot, take the stuff. There's no need to kiss the sod.'

Leggings interpreted the grinning faces as a gesture that everyone was pleased with his magnanimity. Opening the sandbag he was carrying, he handed the Scot a *lempeng* [cake] of golden tobacco with the comment 'Leggie'. There was a considerable sucking-in of breath among some of the men as if they too would have been prepared to take the bashing for such a prize, but the guard had not finished. He tilted the bag and out fell two hands of bananas, pushed by two coconuts. 'Leggie', he chanted, producing a ten-guilder note which he pushed into the flabbergasted man's hand with an action that said he had conferred the ultimate for bravery. Then folding up the sandbag, he tucked it under his arm and walked away. Talk broke out among the men, but for the moment I could not take my eyes from the small pile of fruit and tobacco that represented the price of Leggings' lost face.

Muir stuffed the note in his G-string, smiled at Ringer for his joke, and with a terse 'Help yersels' jumped back into the hole. When the time came for the men on top to spell those in the hole, I told Muir to take the stuff to his hut and put further temptation out of the way.

Bram took several men off to the workshop to con over the pile of timber for the making of a stage, as we had almost reached too great a depth to throw out the spoil. They had just returned with an assortment of poles and planks when Takahashi and the guard commander arrived. The officer started to harangue me and though I knew he was asking why we had abandoned the former location it was beyond my power to explain how electricity had shown where the water was. One of the men was sent to fetch Lieutenant Ringer in the hope that his vocabulary might extend to the subject of water divining.

I told the interpreter about using the wire and how it had indicated that water lay below the spot where we now dug but that there was none where we had first started. I was surprised to see the Jap laugh. Good humour was a phenomenon rarely seen in the man. He nodded his head at the end of the explanation and said, 'You must use your wire to find a well for the guards' camp,' and then asked to see Muir.

Jock had just been to the *benjo* and walked up behind the Jap. He stopped, bowed and then came on. Ringer called out to him that Takahashi wanted a word with him.

The Jap was big, even by European standards, and must have weighed all of 200 pounds. Most of the Japanese were quite short but occasionally one came across a six-footer, mostly employed in the *Kempeitai*.

'Titch' Muir stared up at the smiling face of the towering Jap. Takahashi spoke slowly, pausing to let Ringer interpret sentence by sentence. While pretending to work, everyone listened with interest as the tale was unfolded of how he had heard of Muir's bravery and sportsmanship. Work stopped altogether as the big man spoke of his own prowess as a sportsman, boasting that he needed only two more falls to qualify for the Japanese Olympic judo team. Then what he had been leading up to came out. He wanted to know how a little fellow like Muir could not only take punishment but ask for more, while other prisoners couldn't take it at all.

With a wry grin, Jock told him it was easy. He was a boxer. The Jap did not need an interpreter for the word 'boxer', and to show he understood, put up his fists in mimicry. His smile broadened as he spoke again, asking if Jock would teach his guards to box.

'Not on this grub I won't,' replied the canny Scot.

Ringer spoke and the judo expert nodded his head in appreciation of the position. He told Muir he would get the same food as the guards and be absolved from all working parties if he took the job on. Jock nodded his acceptance. The Jap smiled broadly, pleased with the arrangement, and walked away.

Only laboured breathing and the bite of spades and *chungkals* could be heard as the men returned to their work. Muir leapt into the hole and began to shovel earth.

'Put that down and bugger off,' snapped his friend Storey. 'We don't work with bloody collaborators. Go on, clear off!' The corporal's sentiments were echoed by others who had all stopped working to stare at the pugilist. He dropped the implement as though it were red-hot. There was antagonism in everyone's eyes. He climbed out of the well and walked slowly across the hot, bare ground into the shadow of his hut. He was a hero yesterday, an outcast today.

*Chapter 12*

# The Well

Buck and I worried greatly over the well. The hole was almost twenty-five feet deep with still no sign of water. I began to feel it would have been more profitable had the diggers helped in carrying the stuff from the stream. Water-carrying had to be done all the time we were digging and more shoulders to the tins would have made lighter work of it. Although the ground appeared firm, the shoring was inadequate and the responsibility for men who might be buried under a fall weighed heavily on me. Whatever Buck Sheehy said and however much he cajoled, I decided that tomorrow would be the last day of work on the dry elephant. Had we got to mud I would not have minded, but the place was as dry as the Sahara. The whole affair had become a joke throughout the camp and was spoken of as 'Jennings' Folly'. Even the guards sniggered as powdered earth was brought to the surface.

The men had finished for the day when I told the Queenslander that I intended throwing in the towel if we did not get some sign on the morrow. His face lengthened and I knew he thought of me as one of little faith, but he simply said goodnight and walked away.

My friends were leaving the workshop as I went by.

'No luck, Mick?' called Bram.

I spread out my arms in a gesture of defeat. 'I'll give it tomorrow and no longer. The place is as dry as a bone.'

I felt angry and walked round the camp in the hope of ridding myself of the oppressing gloom. I could see the laughter in Takahashi's eyes when he learned of the failure. The blasted heathen would gloat and perhaps remind me of my electricity. The men who had worked on the project would now tell each other they knew all the time there was no bloody water there.

Dusk was gathering as I walked back. I found myself drawn irresistibly to the great muckheap that Bramble had early on labelled the eighth wonder of the modern world. It had not been half the height at that time, and I had enjoyed the joke. Now his innocent description rankled deeply in my mind. A cloud of dust shot into the air, then another. It could have whipped off the top of the pile had there been any wind, but there was not a whisper. More earth shot into the sky and I hurried forward, wondering what caused it.

Peering down the hole, I saw a bare back straighten as someone lifted a shovelful of earth. A second later I found myself looking at the indistinct features of Bramble. The spoil slipped off the blade and shouting, 'Below!' he grinned up at me and said, 'Hiya Mick.' I heard another muffled voice I recognised as belonging to Ripe Strawberry who had just returned from a working party a quarter of an hour previously.

'Who else is down there?' I asked gruffly, hoping to cover the shame I was feeling.

'Dopey, Grumpy and little Snow White,' laughed Bram, preparing to throw some earth on me. 'Go on, beat it, fellah.' Then one of them began whistling 'Whistle while you work' and I had to duck rapidly to miss the contents of his spade. Moving out of range I sat and waited for the men who had faith to appear. They couldn't go on much longer as night was falling fast, and the supper gong would sound at any minute now.

Then I heard a voice say, 'It's as black as hell down there but I've poked down another couple of feet, bang in the middle.' Buck's head appeared and he was followed by the sergeant major, George and Bram. I got to my feet and went to meet them, feeling chastened by their efforts.

The supper gong sounded.

'Night, Cap'n,' said the Aussie and he and the SM pushed off through the blue–black dusk towards their hut and we returned to ours.

It was still dark when 'Wakey wakey' woke us and half-asleep we stumbled across the parade ground for *tenko*. I called out my number *'hachi hachi nee'* [882], the other officers sneezed and spat theirs, and the guard *'ushed'* us. We ran back to our quarters and breakfast.

As we ate, I suggested to my friends that we concentrate on deepening the central hole that Buck had spoken of the night before, keeping it as small as possible in diameter. They agreed and later we set off to the 'folly', each of us resolute but with me dreading the outcome.

The working party arrived at the same time as we did and I thought it best to tell them that in my opinion the well had become too deep to work in without proper shoring, and only a selected few would be asked to go down. The remainder would be engaged in scattering the spoil around the area and filling in depressions or low-lying ground. The number of men being reported all correct, I queried the SM's statement because the diviner was not present. I asked where Buck was and just then he emerged from between the walls of earth, a large, satisfied grin on his face. It could not possibly have happened, and yet? He saw my questioning look.

'She'll be right, Cap'n. No need to worry anymore.'

'Do you mean, Buck...?'

He nodded happily and as Bram and George shot past me, the party dissolved, men clambering up the miniature mountains of our making to see the phenomenon that had come to pass.

I was incredulous, but Buck assured me it was clear as spring water and coming in full bore. It was there all right, four feet from ground level with all the wooden stages submerged. The relief at seeing the sky reflected in that circular mirror was almost overpowering. I shook hands with the happy Aussie and Ripe Strawberry, congratulating them upon the final effort, then with George and Bram.

Mac lowered a dixie on the end of a piece of rattan, giving it a sharp jag to force the lip under the surface. I was experiencing one of the happiest days I had known since becoming a prisoner of war. The 'folly' had now become 'Jennings' Well' though I referred to it as 'Buck's Bore'.

Bram suggested we needed concrete to surround the well, and with some pipes we could run the water right into the cookhouse as there was plenty of fall. Buck then asked me to request permission to cut the giant bamboo growing close by, and with the tall reeds near the stream outside the perimeter wire, he would make pipes and the legs to support the line.

The colonel was as pleased as I was when I told him of the good fortune we had had at the well and he instantly agreed to accompany me to the guardroom to try and get the things we wanted. It must have been our lucky day, for Takahashi came into the camp while we explained our requirements. Five minutes later we received permission to cut the bamboo. The question of cement was more difficult. Before he could say anything definite he would have to speak with the military engineers. The colonel pressed for this, stressing the danger of typhoid and other diseases that could come from contaminated water.

During the day, the well party brought bamboo galore into camp and Buck began the task of making the pipes. The ingenuity of this man from the Outback was amazing. He skilfully cut a narrow wedge down each length, then knocked out the knots at the join, replaced the wedge and bound it tightly back in place with rattan. Then, with the small end pushed into the large end of the next length, the pipeline began to take shape.

The following day, while more sections were being prepared, others made the supporting legs and the workshop staff completed a box that would be fitted to the upper end of the tiny flume. With two men to feed the box with water, a constant flow should pour into the cookhouse tank. When everything was assembled, all except the water fillers went to watch the opening ceremony of the 'Sungei Ron Water Supply Co.' Water carrying was now a thing of the past. It was another example of what can be done with knowhow and local materials, demonstrated by the joker from the Outback.

A week later, Starting Handle turned up and wanted to know where the cement party was. Very quickly men were rustled up and Bram went out with them. Everyone stepped warily, knowing the guard was one of the vicious types. He had earned his nickname by killing an old Indonesian woman with a starting handle because she had laughed when he had unsuccessfully tried to crank a car engine.

The story Bram told when he got back made unpleasant hearing. To begin with, the cement store was at the far side of the airfield and the bags that had been allocated to us were all hard and lumpy. It was old stuff and would be of little use. Fortunately the guard left the party for a time, and seeing another stack of cement at the other side of the store, Bram poked it and found it to be nice and soft. There was a rapid switch of new for old and a quick reccy for anything that might be useful. Bram's eyes nearly popped out of his head when he found a pile of British RE double-acting pumps. Purloining a couple of them, he opened two bags and buried them in the cement. By the time Handle got back, everyone was sitting innocently watching the rain that had begun to fall. They had been made to wait not because of the effect of rain on the cement but because the guard thought it would soon clear up and he disliked getting wet.

Instead of stopping, the downpour got worse. If they were to get back to camp in daylight, there must be no more delaying, so the Jap ordered the men to march. With their hundredweight loads they went out into the wind-driven rain blowing in their faces. Halfway back, not having had a rest, the men began to flag, and Handle's temper deteriorated as the pace slackened.

'Speedo, speedo!' he roared, urging and threatening them to greater effort. But the near-nude prisoners were only amused by the antics of the curvetting sodden figure. Their worry was the heavy load and the speed at which they were being made to carry it.

Within half a mile of the camp, misfortune struck. Hall, barefooted like most of the others, either slipped or trod on a sharp stone. He stumbled and dropped his bag of cement on the uplifted foot of Storey who walked in the front rank just behind the guard. The corporal was thrown off balance and his load was catapulted into the unsuspecting Handle's back, sending him rolling over and over in the muddy road. Bram, bringing up the rear, was unaware of what had happened until the column stopped, when he stepped to the side and saw the guard picking himself up. My friend ran forward to investigate but was too late to prevent the enraged Jap from jabbing the butt of his rifle into Storey's crotch. It is doubtful whether Bramble could have stopped him anyhow. He would probably have met the same fate himself had he interfered just then. All he could do was stand in the madman's way, hindering him from making a second attack upon the injured NCO who rolled about in agony, his hands between his legs. The guard had to wait in the pouring rain until his victim became mobile again. All his ranting and flourishing of uplifted rifle made no impression on the semi-conscious man.

Bram finally got the corporal to his feet, asked him to do his best to keep up with the party, and shouldered his bag of cement. Moving much more slowly, they started off again. Dusk had thickened into night by the time the camp was reached, and as the front rank stopped inside the gates, Starting Handle lost no time in searching out his lagging victim. With a vicious swipe of his rifle across the NCO's head, he felled him like an ox. Then he went across the road to change his saturated, muddy clothes. The men were dismissed.

Willing hands carried poor Storey to hospital. By the forbidden light of a coconut-oil lamp, the doctor gave one look then slowly shook his head. Everyone in the camp mourned Storey's death and the following morning those not on working parties attended his funeral. Even Muir was there for a while but disappeared as the guard commander placed a basket of fruit on the grave to feed the man's departed soul. Three more prisoners were buried, and the fruit was moved to each grave in turn. It was a Japanese mark of respect that held no real meaning.

After the interments, most of the mourners made their way to the well, splashing through a sea of mud, to prepare the ground for the laying of the concrete surround. I mentioned to Buck that I was surprised to see Muir at the funeral because of their falling out, but Buck had seen Muir's reaction when he heard the news of Storey's death. He just sat staring at the empty place where his old mate used to be. After a time, he began sobbing and shouted out that he would make them pay for this.

A day later the sergeant major came hurrying up all excited and told me to look across at the guard's camp. There we saw the Scot prancing round Storey's killer. Seemingly, it was a normal boxing lesson and some thirty guards sat round the marked square, watching intently, but there was something in Muir's attitude that smacked of the real thing. Suddenly he flashed out a right and left to the face, stopping Handle in his tracks. Clearly angered, the guard tried to kick the professional and paid for the attempt with another smack on the nose we thought we could hear, as Muir danced away. Anyone watching could see that Muir meant business and the blood was flowing freely from Handle's nose and face.

Muir made the game look so easy that the watching guards seemed unable to understand the lethargy of their compatriot. They yelled encouragement to him and he swung wildly, only to totter backwards as hammer blows rained on his face.

Again, Starting Handle attempted to kick the tutor and had to pick himself up off the ground after receiving a blow to the side of the head. Neither rules nor rests were being observed. For fifteen long minutes, the dancing Scot hit the Korean as and when he liked. Suddenly Jock feinted and the guard turned to meet the new attack, leaving his chest unprotected. A large patch of red covered the region of the man's heart as two smashing blows thumped home. The Handle was out on his feet, but as his knees began to sag his head jerked back from a tremendous left hook to the point of the jaw. Storey's murderer lay sprawled in the dust.

Ten minutes later little Jock came into camp. Ignoring the cheers which once again set him on the hero's throne, he went straight to the cemetery and knelt before the grave of his one-time comrade. The sergeant major met him on his way back and, putting out his hand, did his best to wipe out the past. Only for a moment did the little pugilist hesitate, and in the grip that followed, Muir's punishment ceased. He was no longer considered a collaborator.

From that time on, any guard guilty of unwarranted beatings was reported to the wee Scot who, when it came to giving the man his lesson, repeated the tactics he had used on the Handle. It was pleasant to know that we had a means of getting even.

*Chapter 13*

# The Guards

Rarely a week went by when deaths and beatings were not commonplace. One outstanding performance was that of Tor, the Christian guard, who found men of the garden party eating raw root vegetables. These unfortunates were made to stand on the edge of the main road just outside the camp gate. Notices reading: 'I am a thief, spit at me' written in English and *Jawi* [Indonesian] were pinned to their G-strings. Each man held a heavy log above his head and the slightest lowering of arms brought Tor's heavy stick across that individual's shoulders.

Indonesians were not allowed to pass without complying with the notices, while the guards laughingly joined in the game, making special journeys to observe this honourable Japanese custom. Pleas by the colonel against this inhuman treatment were only laughed at. Without food or water, and standing in the blazing sun, the last man collapsed after five hours and was beaten unmercifully as he lay unconscious. All were dragged into camp where we hurried them to hospital.

One evening in the middle of March 1943 the colonel, Bram and I were sitting outside our billets chatting when Starting Handle came along. He said something in Japanese to Colonel Hill who replied that he didn't understand him. Starting Handle then struck him on the face with his clenched fist which sent the colonel staggering backwards. The guard followed him and struck him again on his face with the other fist. Colonel Hill fell to the ground and when he struggled to his feet, Starting Handle punched him again several times on the face. By this time, Hill's face was badly swollen, and blood was pouring from his nose. The beating continued for twenty minutes and then, apparently satisfied, Starting Handle left.

The following day Colonel Hill reported Starting Handle to Japanese HQ and as a result he was taken off guard duties and became Takahashi's chauffeur.

I had my own experience of Starting Handle's form of punishment when about the middle of January 1943 he came into the workshop and demanded I give him the immersion heater I was working on. When I refused, using sign language, he punched me hard in the face and body several times, forcing me against a vice on the workbench. This caused a terrific pain in my back. After I collapsed on the floor he kicked me several times in my ribs and back. As I was trying to get to my feet, Major Lyddon entered, and seeing my condition, assisted me to my bed. Surgeon Cocoron advised me to stay in bed for two days, but on the third day when I returned to work, I had to go back to bed as I found it too hard to stand.

In June 1943, a particularly obnoxious guard nicknamed *Tidak Bagus* [no good] entered the workshop and produced a fountain pen with one of the legs of the nib broken off. He told me that he wanted both legs the same so that he could sell it. I broke the end off the other leg, making them both the same length. Tidak Bagus shouted at me and said that he expected me to put a tiny bit of solder on the broken leg to make them both the same length. He then kicked me several times on my legs and feet. I was wearing wooden clogs and the kicking resulted in my legs and feet being badly bruised.

One afternoon in August 1943, *Tidak Bagus* came into the workshop and attempted to solder a link onto his watch. During this attempt, he badly scorched the face of the watch. He then gave the watch to Bram to finish as he didn't have the skills himself. When Bram gave the watch back to him and Tidak Bagus saw the scorched face, he shouted at Bram in Japanese and jabbed the butt of his rifle into Bram's body. As George and I tried to calm him down he beat both of us with his rifle. Bram was in bed for a week afterwards because of the beating.

It was common to be beaten up for not having a button done up on your tunic (if you owned one). Some of the working parties were beaten up with sticks for sheltering from the rain. Later, a party of 120 men were beaten with the buckle ends of belts for cheering during an air raid.

Incidents, most of them gruesome, often happened, giving everyone plenty to talk about. There was the time when Foster had been brought back into camp by the *Kempeitai* with his testicles festering after having been burned by candles. A few days later he was taken away again and not heard of since. There was Jebson who had been stretched until every joint in his arms and legs had been pulled apart. Many others had once been the subject of pity and conversation, warnings to the rest of us of what Jap frightfulness could be like.

# Chapter 14

# They're Ours

Two more Christmases went by and still the women's camp remained empty. Rank jungle grass covered the land between the huts, making it a paradise for rats and snakes. The thin *attap* roofs had sagged and broken, while forty feet away some thousand civilian men rotted for want of something to do.

Then came the news that some of the women were back and once again I went out with a working party and saw a few bedraggled figures cutting grass near the wire fence. Wearily they waved and again bent to their task. The numbers in the civilian men's camp seemed to be smaller than before but Treverrow and Grandos were still there to watch us go by.

Through the village we went and along the lane to the airfield. The extension to the runway had been completed but we now had to do labouring work for the Jap engineers who were building a control tower and officers' quarters. Hibiscus shrubs had been planted round the whole area, and when the opportunity occurred we stripped them of their leaves and ate them, for even the river weed called *kangkong*, our only vegetable previously, was now denied us. At midday, Ripe Strawberry detailed two men to heat up the ready-cooked rice while the others worked on.

Suddenly there was a shout and the sound of blows being struck, and I hurried from the far end of the line to find the guard using his stick unmercifully on one of the cooks. He turned upon me when I tried to interfere and almost screamed with rage *'Churi! Churi!'* [thief], putting his hand to his mouth and pulling it away quickly as though gobbling something. Then I understood. One of the cooks was Hall and both his fellow worker and the guard had caught him stealing rice. I nodded to the Jap and walked away, hardening my heart to his cries of pain. On one thing, I was determined. He had had all the lunch he would get. I doubted that he would feel like eating anyway when the Jap had finished with him. His incensed comrades even encouraged the Jap with shouts of 'Good boy, Johnny' and 'Let the bastard have it' until I stopped them. The guard looked bewildered at being asked to desist in his punishment of the man for such a heinous crime until I pointed out that he would be punishing those who would have to carry him back to camp if he went on much longer. He saw the point and so did the men. In their anger, it had not occurred to them that he might have to be carried. They were so inflamed that I doubted they would have obeyed an order to pick him up.

When we got to the village on our way back to camp, Hall was fainting and had to be supported. I asked the Jap if he could be given a drink of water to enable him to keep going. The guard readily agreed, realising that if his victim became unconscious part of the punishment would be cancelled. Beckoning the two men who held the thief to follow him, he crossed the road and called to the shopkeeper. An elderly Chinese woman appeared and nervously handed him a small glass of water which he threw into Hall's face and roared an injunction to her to get more and plenty of it.

Timorously the old lady suggested that if the sick man wanted a bath, there was plenty of water in the well behind the shop. Grinning hugely, the Nip nodded that was exactly what he wanted and motioned to the troops again. They disappeared round the corner of the building.

A teenage Indonesian boy came straight towards me. Pushing a packet of cigarettes into my hand, with his eyes on the shop where the party had gone, he whispered rapidly, 'British aircraft come 11 o'clock Tuesday,' and walked away.

Staring after him, I put the packet in my pocket and promptly forgot about it as the laughing guard, troops and a drenched and bedraggled Hall reappeared.

When we passed the internee camps, there seemed to be more women lining the wire. Once more I lagged behind and waved and hoped. Coming to the end of the wire I picked up my place alongside the sergeant major and wondered whether my wife had seen me.

In the gathering dusk, we halted before the guardroom for the usual formality of being searched. I walked behind the guard commander. When he stood before Hall and listened to our guard's explanation, he turned the man around for inspection and, nodding and smiling at the evidence of punishment, dismissed the parade.

Going to the office, I reported the doings of the day. The colonel smiled wryly when I told him about being approached by an Indonesian and his message of bombing at 11 o'clock next Tuesday. I remembered the cigarettes and put the packet on the table. Squinting humorously above the shining gold rims of his spectacles, he looked inside the packet. I knew he wouldn't believe the message, but he said it had given him a laugh and that I'd certainly earned a cigarette. Fumbling, he opened the little cardboard box, and as I took one the orderly brought in his supper. 'Better go and get yours,' he said, 'but for God's sake keep this story to yourself or we shall have men looking up at the sky all day until the Japs want to know what the hell they're doing.'

In my hut, Bram and George wanted to know what was tickling me, but as there were others about, I had to fence and told them how Hall had been beaten up. But when supper was over and we were walking up and down the parade ground, I told them, in the strictest confidence, of the message from the Indonesian. Bram and George immediately started to discuss where the bombers could come from. Unless they were using very different planes from the ones used three years ago, they would have to come from aircraft carriers because of the distance. It wasn't surprising we were all sceptical because we had been fed on rumours for three years, although they both admitted this one was pretty precise.

In the darkness, I heard my name being mentioned. I was told the colonel wanted to see me. Leaving my friends, I walked to the colonel's office where, almost in a whisper, he told me that when giving the rest of the cigarettes to the men in the hospital, he had found a note written in English which said: 'British planes from Cocos will bomb 11 am Tuesday.' He still felt it was a stupid rumour but was horrified at the danger I had been in if I had been searched when returning to camp. A chill crept up my spine at the thought of the execution which would have taken place if the guard had not been interested in Hall and had searched all members of the party. Perhaps by his greed, Hall had unwittingly saved me for a second time.

When George heard the latest news, he pointed out that the distance from the Cocos Islands to Sumatra was about 900 miles. He also considered the return journey without a chance of refuelling. Obviously, he felt it was an impossibility. I ticked them off for their gloomy outlook and noted that we only had to wait three days for the proof! Laughing, we climbed under our rice-sack blankets to dream perhaps of bombs.

The next day we made our usual quota of four bamboo coffins and stripped more material ready for emergencies. There was plenty of room on the bed slats now for everyone. Occasionally one of the workshop staff would relieve the rapidly wasting Panther by taking a burial service for him, though he always insisted on personally writing to the deceased's next of kin, filing the letter for despatch at the first available opportunity. The thirty per cent of surviving prisoners were made to work twice as hard and on decreasing rations to make up for the declining manpower. This existence could not go on much longer. If we continued to lose men at the same rate as over the past year, then nine months would see the extermination of us all. I could only assume that the loss of life in the women's camp was similar to our own. The mental worry about my wife's wellbeing was far worse than my gnawing hunger.

Although I had pretended to be confident about the aircraft coming from Cocos, an awful feeling of depression settled over me as eleven o'clock on Tuesday came and went. Then at midday, Bramble, having noticed my melancholy, suddenly remembered what day it was and that zero hour had come and gone. Even the colonel came over to point out that my Indonesian informant was nothing more than a rumour-monger and that I might have lost my head through his damned nonsensical melodramatics.

After lunch, I was battering flat a piece of corrugated iron to make another drumming-up tin for one of the men, when a clap like thunder shook the earth. *Strange*, I thought, as there was no rain.

Putting down the hammer, I went to the door just in time to see the perimeter wire disappear. In the sky I could see the small specks of the raiding force and my heart jumped with joy.

'They're ours!' roared Bram in my ear as the air raid siren shrilled.

I yelled back, 'Look at that time! It's one o'clock Tokyo time and eleven o'clock by God's time!'

He stared at the sundial upon which he himself had painted 'TT'. 'By hell you're right! They're bang on!'

The khaki-clad figures of guards came pouring across the road making for their funk hole positions round the camp, yelling furiously to the prisoners to get under cover. It was not with any thought for our safety that they shouted their orders. Palm-thatched huts would have been no use against the heavy bombs which were falling over by the airfield and on the oil installations at Bukit Tinggi, sending flames and columns of black smoke high into the clear blue sky. They were afraid that the hysterically happy men might take matters into their own hands. Indeed, had the troops known that almost all the Jap rifles were non-lethal they might easily have done so. The enemy might also have been afraid of the cameras the aircraft carried but even if no photographs of the cheering troops were taken, the lines of tattered washing would be sufficient to tell anyone it was a prisoner-of-war camp. From such a height, all three camps would appear on the negative and each would show the unmistakeable sign of a bamboo hell.

Billowing clouds of smoke at the airfield told us why no aircraft had attempted to go in pursuit. Scared Japs screamed loudly, presumably trying to maintain quiet among the troops, but gave it up as a bad job when the men in one hut started singing 'There'll always be an England', to be followed by hut after hut until the whole camp was singing it. The song did not finish until the All Clear sounded and begrimed sentries climbed from their funk holes and went back to the guardroom, too scared to interfere with men whose patriotism had reached fever pitch. Catcalls and shouts of 'changey-changey' followed them as they scurried past the huts.

I found the colonel watching the smoke clouds piling up and up. With difficulty I kept my face straight as I greeted the old Indian soldier. 'Did you hear all that thunder, sir?'

'Thunder?' he boomed, then caught the twinkle in my eye. 'All right, Jennings, I'll grant you it came off, even if it was late.'

But I reminded him that we were two hours ahead, being on Tokyo time, and that the bombers were dead on time. The colonel was floored and realised he had forgotten this fact. Then the tired soldier gulped as if to rid himself of the emotion which threatened to overwhelm him again.

'I was afraid these little yellow bastards might shoot at the cheering men. It's bad enough to see the sick die so near the end, but to be shot after all they have gone through would be the last straw.'

That was the moment I told the colonel about the secret the workshop staff had kept for three long years, as Chisy had done with his radio. I reassured the colonel now the end was near that every rifle fitted with a copper swivel had its firing pin filed. His brow furrowed as he thought of the implications if we had been caught. Then he smiled and admitted he was glad he didn't know but we had no doubt made the changeover much safer.

That evening, just before roll call, orders were posted that no parties would leave camp the next morning and everyone was jubilant. Those who had been out of camp during the raid came back with stories of how a stick of bombs had fallen right along the airstrip and others had plastered the hangars, making a fine mess of the whole show. The wood-chopping party had been made to lie down with their faces to the ground, but when the guard had done so everyone turned over and enjoyed watching the bombs fall.

The following morning from dawn until breakfast time a stream of lorries poured into camp. As soon as the meal was over every man who could get on his feet was ordered into one or other of the vehicles. Twenty minutes later we stood on the airfield, surveying the damage that had been done by our bombers. Small hills surrounded craters on what had once been the runway, while over the far side of the field the blackened ruins of two hangars still gave off wisps of blue smoke. Nearby, the control tower on which we had spent so many hours labouring to mix concrete leaned drunkenly to one side, leaving the steel reinforcement standing stark and bent against the sky. One of the petrol dumps had exploded and empty drums littered the area.

A company of Jap engineers took command and soon every man was at work with *chungkal*, shovel or wheelbarrow, filling in the craters. Lashes and blows were frequent as they drove both officers and men. Admittedly the Japs worked hard themselves, but they did not seem to understand why the starving prisoners could not equal their capacity. At first they were clearly under the impression that we were working to a go-slow policy, which angered them beyond all measure. Then as one man after another collapsed, the true reason dawned on them and an issue of concentrated sugar-water was provided with the midday rice.

At dusk, flares were lit and we had visions of having to work on through the night. It was long past the normal dinnertime and the reason for the further sweetened water we had been given at five o'clock was now clear. At eight o'clock the whistle sounded and we were ordered to fall in and return to camp. Another crowd of men began taking up the tools we had so gladly thrown down and I smiled to catch the momentary gleam of Treverrow's red beard. The internees were being given a job at last! Thirteen hours after leaving camp we returned on foot, too tired to eat even the scanty meal that awaited us.

For three days and in ever-diminishing numbers, the party worked a twelve-hour stint at the airfield before life was allowed to resume the normal rhythm of one day on and one day off.

I went out with the Saturday airfield party in order to get two consecutive days' rest, Sunday being a rest day for everyone did not count. Passing the women's camp, I lagged behind as usual to stare at the faces which had become much more blurred now and I hoped I had been seen by my wife. The bombing raid had put much more verve into the women's cheering, and with a lighter heart I regained my position in the ranks after we had passed by. The whistling these days had become spasmodic and by the time we reached the village it had almost petered out.

All day long we pushed drums of water to the places where the craters had been, emptying them out and returning for more. Occasionally the water fatigue changed places with the men who filled in the depressions made by heavy road rollers which the Japs were using to consolidate the ground. The strip was useable for fighter aircraft by the time we left.

## Chapter 15

# Changi, Singapore

We weren't to know what our captors had in mind for us now that it seemed the tide was turning in our favour. Early on the morning of 26 May 1945, we were informed that we were to be ready to leave the camp, taking only the minimum of possessions.

We were lined up after *tenko* and 99 of the officers and 1,000 men (one of whom was a man named Lord who had one leg and walked with the assistance of a crutch) were marched three miles in the heat of the day to the dock at the Moesi River. Those of us who could walk helped the weaker men as we stumbled through the dust, carrying our few meagre bundles of pots, pans and rags of clothing.

Once at the dock we boarded a steamer of around 1,200 tons and were told we were bound for Singapore. Conditions were appalling as we were forced to sleep on deck, all of us crammed onto a hatch about twenty-five feet square. It was utterly impossible for any of us to sit or lie down. The men were in the same position as the officers, and as the decks were made of iron, they became unbearably hot during the day.

Food consisted of rice and very little of it, and we were issued a few bananas cooked with their skins on. With only an allowance of less than half a pint of water per day per head, many collapsed and were only held up by the crush of bodies. After about three days at sea, two of the men went raving mad. The journey to Singapore took four days, during which we were fully exposed to the sun with no quarters or shade.

On arrival, we were all conveyed in trucks to Changi Gaol. We found conditions here a great improvement on the camp in Sumatra. Although work parties were still being sent out to labour on airfields and in other areas, we knew a change was in the air as extra rice rations were distributed and our clandestine radio reports gave us hope that the end was near.

We heard officially on 15 August that the ceasefire order had been given and on 18 August the Korean guards were told that it was all over. The Japs said we could send another of the meagre postcards home! No doubt they were hoping the improved conditions would be reported and they would be looked upon kindlier in the months to come.

In September we were issued with clean new clothes, which caused much merriment. Everyone could have worn small size clothing but when that had all been issued, medium and outsize garments, provided by thoughtful statisticians, turned the men into a crowd of laughing clowns.

'If yer mother could only see you now!' was the constant remark, as small men roamed the camp in ankle-length shorts and baggy shirts. The camp accordionist added to the cheer by playing 'There'll always be an England'.

'Didn't know you with your clothes on, sir,' said the sergeant major with a grin, eyeing the shredded ends of my new shorts which had been reduced to reasonable proportions with the aid of the tin snips.

When Red Cross parcels were distributed, one per man, the Japs enjoyed a restricted popularity with the forgiving troops until they were opened. Cigarettes and chocolate that had not been eaten by white ants were green with mildew. Hats and socks had suffered from the depredations of cockroaches and were useless. Tins of yeast extract were still in good order and these were handed in to the cookhouse to be used communally. In some of the parcels, packers had put a chit wishing the recipient good luck, with the date 1941. A party of our own men was sent to investigate the stocks of Red Cross supplies and returned with the staggering news that there were 62,000 parcels and that they had been in the godown since 1942.

The Jap and Korean guards vanished overnight and when on Monday 3 September the Union Jack was hoisted up the masthead at the gaol, we felt we could finally release the pent-up excitement and believe our horrendous time was almost over. The surrender ceremony took place with an announcement by Lord Mountbatten on Wednesday 12 September at the Municipal Building of Singapore and our years of suffering were ended.

My joy was tempered by the feeling that my beloved wife, Margery, might still be incarcerated in Sumatra, or worse, not have survived her terrible ordeal. My last letter from her told me that she was in the camp hospital and although she sounded brave and cheerful, I could tell her health was failing.

I was walking down the street in Singapore shortly after leaving Changi and met a woman who had been in Margery's camp. I asked her for news of my Midge and if she knew what had happened to her. She replied quite casually, 'Oh she died.' Her blunt words were a terrible shock to me, but I could understand her reply because after all the deaths and suffering and the complete exhaustion emotionally and physically, she must have had little sympathy left to deliver such news more softly.

The British Military Administration (BMA) had made Raffles Hotel the headquarters for sorting out the prisoners who had survived. The Japanese had kept few records of those held in camps or who had died, so this mammoth task relied mostly on survivors' information.

I was sitting in Raffles when I was approached by a quiet, gentle woman who had been in camp with Margery. She introduced herself as Elizabeth (Pip) Meyer and said she knew I was Margery's husband the minute she saw me sitting there. She explained how she and Margery became fast friends and how much the friendship meant to her. She recounted the day Margery found out that I was alive, following my escape attempt. She told me how Margery turned to her with tears in her eyes and thanked her Father in Heaven that I was alive and in Palembang.

Pip gave me Margery's wedding ring, notebook and Bible, together with my gold cigarette case, which she had never sold for food although she was in such dire need. I learnt of my beloved's last days and how Pip had comforted her and been with her till the end. My brave Midge had spent her time supporting others and being the best she could be in that grave situation, her love of music helping her through the worst of times.

In memory, I saw again those far-off days when I had lain helpless in hospital and been transported by the vision of those golden curtains. Now I drew comfort that my darling Midge had passed through those heavenly curtains.

I had been delivered from evil, but at what a cost.

## Weights Recorded In Bencoolen Hospital

|  | JENNINGS | HALL |
| --- | --- | --- |
| 8 Sept 1942 | 96lb 8oz | 118lb 8oz |
| 14 Sept 1942 | 93lb 5oz | 129lb 8oz |
| 21 Sept 1942 | 97lb 9oz | 125lb 4oz |
| 28 Sept 1942 | 92lb 4oz | 121lb 0oz |
| 5 Oct 1942 | 90lb 2oz | 127lb 6oz |
| 12 Oct 1942 | Too ill to be weighed | 138lb 6oz |
| 19 Oct 1942 | 99lb | 140lb 4oz |
| 26 Oct 1942 | 104lb 6oz | 147lb 4oz |
| 2 Nov 1942 | 107lb 8oz | 149lb 6oz |
| 1941 | 156lb | 171lb |
| Max loss | 65lb 8oz | 52lb 2oz |
| Age | 42 | 28 |
| Height | 5ft 7in | 5ft 9in |

The last mention of Treverrow comes in the form of a report, reminding us that the freed prisoners were still in danger from Indonesians fighting for independence from the Dutch.

### REPORT BY CAPTAIN JW SMITH, R.A., ON INCIDENT
### MONDAY 5<sup>TH</sup> NOVEMBER 1945 AT BENKOLEN
[misspellings are original]

A party consisting of Captain J Mockler, I.A.M.C., Captain J W Smith, R.A, Driver-Mechanic Jackson, Lincs – regt. and Mr Treveroe [Treverrow], ex-British Civilian Internee, left Palembang on Saturday, 3<sup>rd</sup> November 45, proceeding by road in two cars to Lahat and Benkolen [Bencoolen] for inspection of hospitals and medical stores, and also for me to collect and escort RAPWI personnel at Bencoolen to Palembang.

We left Palembang at 1200 hours on Saturday 3<sup>rd</sup> Nov and travelled to Lahat by road, arriving at 2230 hours and spent the night at the Residency. The journey was entirely without incident. On the morning of the 4<sup>th</sup> we arranged to have all medical stores laid out for inspection on return journey in a few days. We left Lahat at 1015 hours making our way by road to Loeboek Linggau, where we arrived without incident and collected personal belongings of a party of ex-Internees who came from there two days previously. We continued our journey and en route from Loeboek Linggau to Bencoolen. Captain Mockler's car broke a half-shaft and was left with Jackson at KEPALATIOEROEP 69 kilos from Bencoolen 2200 hours without incident. On the morning of the 5<sup>th</sup> Captain Mockler saw the Director of Jap Medical Services and I saw the Jap Military Officers, advising them of our intentions to round up and evacuate RAPWI in that area to Palembang. Some RAPWI families were in hospital and there was a rumour that another two Eurasian families were in the vicinity of Bencoolen.

At 1000 hours on the 5<sup>th</sup> we left Bencoolen to investigate and if possible, to collect these families for evacuation. We proceeded quite slowly in a northerly direction and about two miles out of town we ran into a large road block with about 100 natives. I pulled up at the road block and as I stopped, Mr Treveroe got out to talk to the natives. At the same time, Captain Mockler seemed also to have opened his door and left the car then turned back, presumably to pick up cigarettes or something. I was still in the driving seat and the first indication that I had that anything was wrong was when the Doc suddenly yelled, 'Oh Jesus'. I turned in my seat and saw him turn away from the car with a spear in his back. I got out my gun but immediately my thumb was cut to the bone by a knife which caused me to drop the gun. I fought my way against the spears and left the car by the near-side door. As I left the car, the Doc went down with the natives still thrusting at him. I fought my way round to the front of the car where Treveroe was making his stand but by the time I reached him he also was dead. I was now completely ringed with spears and decided there was no future in remaining so made a break for it. I succeeded in getting so close to the natives that their spears and knives were useless because they were so densely packed. I managed to break through the ring and then dashed in amongst the native houses. I reached the sea and ran into it for about 70 yards until the water was up to my chin. The natives gathered on the shore and used my exposed head as target for my own gun. I remained there for about ten minutes undecided whether to swim to Bencoolen or return in case the Doc was not dead. The natives seemed calmer by this time, so I risked coming out of the sea.

I was immediately seized, my arms bound in front of me and all my personal belongings were stripped, and I was then led up the road to the scene of the fighting. The bodies of Captain Mockler and Mr Treveroe had been pulled into the side of the road and completely stripped. The natives surrounded me with spears and the leader came up to me and shouted 'Nica, Nica' [Netherland Indies Civil Administration?]. I shouted back just as loud 'I am not, you B... B...'. I then asked if anyone spoke English. After standing in the middle of the road, bound for about ten or fifteen minutes, a car approached from the direction of Bencoolen and a native who seemed to have some authority came out of the car and approached me. I immediately said, 'Do you speak English?' He said yes, so I asked that he free my hands and take me back to Bencoolen to the so-called Indonesian Resident Tjaija (sp). He gave no reply but walked on to where the leader of the gang was standing. He then proceeded to argue, pointing to the bodies and then to me and then came back towards me. I asked him again to release me. His reply was to point to the bodies and say, 'This must be kept quiet'. I then said, 'You are a bigger B... than you look'. He went. I was then led back to the beach and the remainder of the rope, about 20ft. long, was wrapped round and round me to ensure I was securely bound. Fortunately, they only bound the upper part of my body and by straining against the rope while being bound I managed to keep it reasonably slack. When they had finished this I was held by a native holding the end of the rope, about a yard long, and was guarded by eight spearmen. They then started to dig my grave on the beach and about the same moment a middle-aged native appeared with a short sword and started walking towards me. Once again, I decided it was a case of now or never, so bowled the native holding the end of the rope against the nearest spearman and escaped into the sea. This time I did not hesitate but diversed [divested] myself of the rope and my clothes and started swimming to Bencoolen, a distance of approximately two miles.

After swimming for about half an hour, nearly halfway, an outrigger made upon me whereupon I surface-dived and swam under the water for as long as possible. This was repeated three times and then the last time I surfaced I came under the bows of a second boat of whose approach I was not aware. In it were two Indonesian policemen who invited me to come aboard. I was extremely dubious of this and insisted on hanging on to the outrigging only. They seemed harmless on closer inspection and eventually I climbed on to the stern of the boat. They invited me to the middle of the boat which I refused. I then insisted that they take me to Bencoolen which they agreed to do in the end, and I was handed over to Mr Ating, Indonesian Commissioner of Police under the old Dutch regime.

I was then put into the hands of a Jap doctor and a Chinese Doctor Lee who found I had ten wounds from spears and knives; they dressed them and made me comfortable. While my wounds were having preliminary dressing at the police station, the Indonesian Resident Tjauja (sp) came in and I demanded the return of all our personal belongings, including the car, and also asked him to accompany the police for the recovery of the bodies. None of our personal belongings were returned.

6th Nov 45                    (Sgd) Captain _____ RA

# BOOK THREE

# Margery's Diary

JANUARY 1942, Singapore

19 January    *Celeste went away.*

20 January    *Bad blitz near Kandang Kerbau Hospital. Play for wedding 5 pm.*

21 January    *Blitz. Visit Wilson, hospital. 5 pm. Intercession.*

22 January    *Blitz each day now. Choir practice.*

23 January    *K.K. Hospital.*

24 January    *Wedding 2.30 pm.*

25 January    *Sunday. S. S. Church. Church Radio Service. Sang 'Oh rest in the Lord'.*

29 January    *K.K. Hospital. No choir.*

30 January    *Many Methodist missionaries sailed for Java including Bishop and Mrs Lee. Hobart injured in groin. Mabel left. Cyril [Mick] returned; we removed to the Hinches'.*

31 January    *Causeway [linking Singapore and Malaya] blown up. Played two Cathedral weddings.*

Margery and Mick had been close friends with the Hinches. As noted above, they went to stay with the Hinches on January 30 and Mr Hinch and Mick finally made the decision as to when the women should try to escape on February 11. Due to her serene and powerful personality, Gertrude Hinch was always referred to respectfully as Mrs Hinch in camp. In the face of the angry rants of the Japanese, she responded calmly and smiled at them, defusing the situation, an admirable skill.

On one occasion a neurotic Japanese nicknamed Ah Fat waddled through camp, concerned about a trivial matter such as the British cooking fires.

He yelled at the top of his voice 'Inchi! Inchi!' for Mrs Hinch. She sailed out of the hut calmly with a bored but dignified expression on her face and while the rest of the women cracked up, asked him coolly what he wanted.

On 26 February, Margery notes: *Short service, 'Ye having nothing yet possess all things' (Lent).* I can't imagine how the women coped with that idea. Another woman in camp, Peggy Starns, wrote: 'Before camp I led a very sheltered, privileged life. In camp, there was no privacy. You couldn't go into a room and shut the door. I mixed with all sorts of people and it made me understand them and feel in the future that I could mix with everybody. I was so much more trusting of human nature than when I went in.'

Some women felt free to be themselves. The strictures of class and position or just of being a wife had gone. You could express yourself openly. You could be who you were. After camp, you were less free.

It was like leaving your life behind, like being on holiday in a strange way, with none of the routines or bills to pay and nothing to plan. Life just went from day to day. There was no one to help so the women fixed everything themselves and became a lot more resourceful.

They were still getting help from the Dutch at this point. Margery writes: *News, if not merely **rumour**, is better of naval battles. Dutch consul presented a pig, bless him. Rice and fish for the evening meal. Tried my brains on a crossword.*

*We were all upset by the **rumour of an officers' club to be opened and women wanted!!** Good heavens. Nothing doing here unless it's above board. Sold gold bangles for 50 guilders.*

Margot Turner, another PoW, commented on the Officers' Club idea, noting that the only way to avoid attention from the Japanese was for the nurses to make themselves look as ugly as possible. 'In the early days, the Japanese tried to get some Australian nurses to go to a nightclub but of course they just dressed themselves up in all sorts of things and put mud on their faces to make them look very unattractive,' wrote Penny Starns.

The nurses put on their military uniforms and others just covered themselves up as much as possible. They wore boots, plimsolls and Wellingtons. Some went with dirty bare feet. Some teased their hair and others pulled it back in a severe ponytail.

The women arrived in a group because they had decided there was safety in numbers. A couple of English male prisoners went with them, but this was more for moral support because there was little they could do.

There were six Japanese officers, two in one house and four in another. Waiters served biscuits and liquor; sugar and little cakes were placed on the tables. Conversation was desultory, needless to say. None of the women drank the liquor so the Japanese asked them what they drank. They replied, 'Milk'. The nearest the Japanese could get to milk was soft drinks. While the women stuffed the cakes and sugar into their pockets, refusing a shopping trip to town to buy cosmetics, they were terrified the Japanese would turn on them. But after two hours the charade ended.

## APRIL 1942

In her diary, Margery writes: *First thing in the morning we were told to leave our houses with clothes and food. I had to leave my second suitcase and just carried bundles and one suitcase. Bob and the men were sent to the other place [prison]. We were marched to houses near where we had lived at first, now thirty-three of us in an empty house with no water or light. I'm glad our group of women are still together. Had a dreadful night with mosquitoes.*

Margot Turner remembers: 'They had got these houses that would normally house four people now housing about sixteen or twenty. You slept on the floor, and in those early days they used to bring rations in... When one looks back, those early days which seemed pretty awful were really the better days because the civilians were looking after us.'

*The next day I arose very early. Saw the moon as a crescent and a gorgeous dawn, which beautified my whole day. Had a bath, also washed my clothes. May I learn patience; we are all getting weak and easily exhausted. There's a rumour that the international situation is good. Walked in the evening before bedtime.*

## MAY 1942

*Heard more gunfire. Sat admiring the moonlight and chatting at night. God bless you, my Mickey. Many officers are around the camp and some patients taken to [Charitas] hospital while some returned. Afterwards May and I went to the garage to a reading led by Miss Cullen. Sang one hymn to 'Londonderry Air'. Happy atmosphere there. There was a free fight in the back bedroom while I was out! Hear planes in the night – very hopeful sound.*

Helen Colijn describes the hospital trips: 'The Japanese allowed us to go for medical visits to the Charitas Hospital in Palembang. It was still staffed by Dutch Franciscan nuns, and Dutch Dr Peter Tekelenburg was in attendance. His wife and two daughters were with us in the women's camp. Once a week a wheezy old ambulance, its innards removed, called at our camp to pick up patients put on the Charitas list by our camp doctor, Jean McDowell.'

Jean was another interesting character in the camp. She had a soft Highland accent and a calm direct manner that the Japanese seemed to respond to, much like Mrs Hinch. She always carried a bag of medical supplies with her. Norah Chambers noted she was a fine character and remembered her curls piled on top of her head as a symbol of optimism.

The nuns took care of the local people, the women's camp and the men internees in Palembang gaol. The Japanese ordered the three groups not to mix but Mother Alacoque maintained a courier system between the men and women, hiding notes in her voluminous habit. The women sewed the notes into the hem of their shorts or in the straps of sun-halters and when they returned to camp they delivered the notes. It was a risky game to play. At one point the Japanese caught Mother Alacoque smuggling notes. She was interrogated and tortured by the *Kempeitai* and put into solitary confinement for some months.

Margery records her daily life: *Had a singsong at the garage. Sang 'On Ilkla Moor Baht 'at', 'To a Miniature', and 'As I Sit Here'. Nice time. On Sunday rations arrived at service time. I began my week of helping distribute the vegetables. New potatoes today but no meat. Wet through, so bathed early.*

Betty Jeffrey, an Australian Sister, describes a musical evening: 'Every Saturday night the Sisters living next door give community singing concerts for all and sundry to air their lungs. These concerts have improved each week and now the variety of items could not be improved upon. English Mrs Jennings, with a glorious voice, sings many songs; we make her sing 'Little Silver Ring' more than others. Mrs Jennings plays the piano well and cheers us up by playing everything we know so we can sing to our heart's content. Miss Dryburgh, an English missionary, plays accompaniments for the camp's best singers, Mrs Murray, Mrs Jennings, Mrs MacLeod and Mrs Chambers, who are all very generous with their glorious voices. Miss Dryburgh or Mrs Jennings conducts the singers and their efforts are really marvellous. How everybody enjoys it!'

## JUNE 1942

*Visited Mrs Gray and had my shoes stuck together once more. Another good curry. Walked a little, chatted on the verandah and sang Gilbert & Sullivan with Sylvia. A hawker was caught today. Washed my hair today and prepared part of Sunday talk.*

Helen Colijn, in the same camp, noted that a Chinese hawker was caught throwing a loaf of bread over the wire behind the Australians' hut. The guards pulled him into the camp and tied him to a pole. 'They raised his arms above his head and tied a rope to his hands and neck in such a way that it would strangle him when he lowered his arms.' It took the man three days to die in full view of the children in the camp. No one was allowed to help him although they tried. It's surprising Margery didn't mention it in her diary.

Margery continues to count off the weeks: *Nineteen weeks since we left Singapore. In the evening visited and walked with Dorothy Moreton, nice to chat about old Methodist Mission friends. Beautiful moonlight night. Bless you Mickey darling, my prayers are with you.*

She mentions walking with friends in the evening. Helen Colijn describes it as being like tigers in a cage, pacing back and forth, back and forth, four houses on each side of the road, exchanging rumours. Even President Roosevelt said the troops would be home by Christmas. Now *that* was a rumour worth hatching out!

All the music had to be remembered and written out. Margery notes she wrote out hymn verses for the service: *Practised Te Deum. Was asked to conduct a choral group. Miss Dryburgh is to write harmonies. Mrs Chambers will write out the manuscript. Agreed. Sang solo at singsong.*

*Song practice at No. 7 at 11 am, quite promising. New list required. Arranged for Mavis to get Klim [milk powder] if possible. Gave her 30 dollars for same. Spoke to Marie re making a new dress.*

## JULY 1942

*Early morning, I was taken to hospital in the hard van. Surprised to find so little attention and such Dutch preference. Dr Anna Goldberg very friendly and good. Allowed warm tea and soup. Thirteen in the room. Regret being placed next to a T.B. case. Can see the only advantage here will be to feed up on what we buy.*

Interestingly, Dr Goldberg was German but also Jewish, which meant the Japanese weren't quite sure whether to call her an ally or not. As a result, she was careful to be as neutral as possible with her many patients. In the last days of Irenelaan [Palembang] in September 1943, the Charitas Hospital was closed down and the only doctor remaining, Dr Goldberg, was sent to the women's camp.

## AUGUST 1942

Memorable day. News of Mick. Was amazed to find Norry and Mick had been together in Sumatra until May. Intensely interested to hear their adventures at sea and on land. Not surprised they eventually parted company, as CO would not be priest-minded. But later in conversation with Mr Green (another) who was with Mick in the smaller party, learned the reason of division. During stay in hospital also contacted another (Captain Thorlby, RE) of the original party. All had malaria. Very thrilled over adventures and although at first thought Mick must now be imprisoned in Sumatra because he and Hall were reported taken after their boat had smashed between Kroe and Bencoolen, can get no confirmation of imprisonment or the names of men said to be captured.

All three whom I contact speak of Mick as though he's still free and will attain his object (reaching Australia in a small boat with Bombardier J. Hall). Gist of the news I gleaned was Mick left Malaya after Singapore fell, the following day in fact, in a junk. Sailed up the Indragiri River. At Ayer Molek, Thorlby and Padre Rowles first met him. Later met again at Padang, which did not fall to the Japs until 16 March.

A party of them left just before the Japs came in. Had many sea adventures on islands and in small boats. First went to Sipoera [Sipura] Island. Last 36 hours of voyage Mick ate leaves (mangrove) which poisoned him, so was in a nasty mess. Four days on Sipura until Mick recovered.

Left for Pulau Pagai on 24 March, arrived next day. Met party of Dutch, Belgian and Mr Ingles (English) people from Batavia. On 27 March party divided into two. COJ, Green and Bomb. Hall in one – Padre, Thorlby and others in bigger party. Obtained boats and provisions.

1 April for island of Enggano. CO's party very slow, arrived twenty-fourth; other party arrived on the eighth. Green last saw Mick on the twenty-seventh as he (Green) then joined other party at Malakoni, needing medical treatment. Heard COJ and J. Hall left Enggano on fourth or fifth of May [actually 1 May].

Later in the month COJ and JH are said to have been captured and boat smashed between Kroe and Bencoolen. Padre's party learned of this at Bencoolen where they were taken as prisoners on 12 July, but could not trace COJ's capture, as he was not imprisoned there. Later they were brought to Palembang. All the party had suffered extremely from malaria.

Said COJ was well when last seen. Captain Thorlby spoke glowingly of COJ and from each of them I received an impression of COJ's courage.

How I rejoice to have news of Mick even though his present circumstances are obscure. Do at least know he was alive until May and got away from that Singapore inferno after all hope had gone and she had capitulated. God bless and keep you, Mickey darlingest.

Twenty-six weeks since I left Singapore. My weight 58kg (9 stone 2lb).

## OCTOBER 1942

Having a strong belief was very important for some women. Ena Murray said her belief became the most important thing in her life. She had been religious only in a perfunctory sense in her previous life but in camp it stopped her from feeling forsaken. Miss Dryburgh's services were a huge compensation together with the friendship of others. Sister Catherina noted they didn't have much time to pray but she felt a trust that God was near and this gave you strength to go on. Norah Chambers felt being fatalistic helped her. She just accepted what came day by day. Optimism and the will to live served her well.

The structure of church services and the concomitant music was also a help. Margery played the piano every day at this point and the choir practices were relentless. Writing poems and music were familiar and 'civilised' things to do. Letters to friends and family continued, whether they got through or not.

## NOVEMBER 1942

5 November – 38 weeks since we left Singapore. Church choir practice, also one for St Andrew's night. Practice for principals in operetta. Observed Remembrance at No. 7 with my Australian friends. Obtained their addresses.

*Armistice Day 11 November.* 'We had an impromptu service in our house conducted by Sister Jean Aston and Mrs Jennings. We all wore our ragged uniforms with limp white collars, but as we haven't any footwear, we were barefooted. The service was a bit harrowing and I think we were all glad when it was over.' *(Betty Jeffrey)*

Music became increasingly important. Three or four months into their internment, routines and structures were being put in place as hope of liberation faded and boredom set in.

Helen Colijn wrote: 'The concerts, teas, charades, lectures and lessons all reflected the interests of the leisure-class women that most of us had been. These leisure activities kept us sane in the crushing boredom of internment, just as domestic skills – the womanly skills – kept us alive.' She mentions lectures on butterfly collecting, astronomy, rubber harvesting and anything people had experienced. Some learned languages, some learned to sew.

## DECEMBER 1942

Special red-letter day 1 December. Received news of my darling Mick being here in Palembang military camp. It is a marvel he survived 127 days at sea with Hall in small boat. No sight of land, boats or aircraft – forty days' food, twenty days no food, then caught a seagull, ate raw, and lived on seagulls afterwards. Some days had none. Once caught eight in one day. What must surely have saved them was their forty-gallon water tank which the rain kept filled (Providence again). Boat broken and dashed against rocks in the breakers near Bencoolen. CO was wearing ring and wristwatch, Hall wearing ring and tattered shirt. Spent the night in gaol and then went to hospital. Mick weighed only 98lb.

Thank God you have come through, my darling. How amazing you should be brought to Palembang after all this time, and how great a relief for you to know me safe, even as for me to know you alive and well. Had note from Norry Cook today telling the great news too. As CO has only been here since the evening of 29 November, I have been exceedingly favoured to hear of him so soon. Can imagine the reception he received from his fellow officers. Norry writing and trying to advise and send discreet news. Surely my faith has been justified this day. Had a restless night after such exciting news.

Amazing news of whispering annoyance [in hospital]. Am confident Mick is as sane as ever, if not **more** so.

Received three letters from Mick. Poor Mick having to put up with whispering campaign of auto-suggestion. His third letter never saner or dearer.

Betty Jeffrey: 'At Christmas time the camp choral society, consisting of both British and Dutch women, gathered on the verandah of House No. 2, where they were joined by almost everybody else in camp. This was the only spot in the camp where women could see their relatives in the distance each morning and evening. The men were building themselves a camp about a mile or so away. They were marched from the jail to this camp every morning and back each afternoon. On the way, they passed this spot where we could see them; they were about 400 yards away from us. Each time they passed they would stop and wave, then go on again. This day they waved, and the women sang to them 'O Come All Ye Faithful'. They stopped dead and listened, then when we finished, waved hankies, shirts and hats, and we heard an echo of 'Thank you'. Two days later they stopped at the same corner and sang to us, the same hymn in English and then in Dutch. Everyone wept.'

**Boxing Day:** Ambulance arrived for over-needy cases. Took the lead at CUC. I received two marvellous letters from Mick dated the eighth and twenty-third. Contents were such as I had become sceptical of ever hearing, though constantly praying for him. Learned of CO's faith and how it had been his mainstay during the voyage and since; of how he had prayed for me and himself; of vow to go to church every Sunday – of belief it was direct answer to prayer he was saved and brought here – of it being indeed a miracle. God be praised, my Mickey. I am overjoyed for you and for myself. We have the world before us – a joint outlook and a great love, plus the greatest love of all. Wrote to Mick telling him how it had gladdened my heart and soul. Too wonderful after all these years. My prayers as well as his have been answered. Cannot express my joy or the loveliness of getting this most longed-for news here in an internment camp. Our privations have been worth it, and we have found God and ourselves and a greater strength through faith than ever before as Mick finds it has brought him consolation and happiness as never before. Told a few of my most understanding friends later, but not that day.

## MARCH 1943

We were promised better rations. Feb and Nov letters from civvies arrived. Told we shall be given 400gm of vegetables as against the present ludicrous one. Felt rather sad early and late evening. Longing for a letter from Mick. Needing money too.

*Sold gold necklace to Kong ($15) and sent jade beads to hospital to sell. Sent message to COJ via Norry and others that I now need money. Very joyful to find Norry had sent 10 guilders for me and Smithy and that it was handed to her in the morning, so it had been sent before getting my message. He will be very happy to know it came at such a needy time. Lucille received gift of hen eggs from her aunt and insisted on giving me two, so I went to her room to eat them (boiled) – very good. All in all, a very pleasing day. Went to CUCs. Mrs Sammy spoke on Vienna old and new right up to the present war. Was interested in her viewpoint of Austria's plight after the last war and now. Made mock sausages from brown beans.*

*Practising for concert. Great Bear [a guard] helped with removal. Half the camp attended in the evening. Very successful concert. Much appreciated (Schubert and Haydn plus Irish and light songs). I sang 'A Little House' by Haydn. Played Haydn's String Quartet as a duet with Miss Dryburgh. Played Schubert piano solos. Accompanied Mick Syers in 'Here is my Heart'. Sang in trios 'Ave Maria' and 'Serenade', also duet 'Juanita' and conducted choral items.*

*Repeated the concert in the evening to the other half of the camp; much enjoyed. Miss Prouse in Chair. Dr Mac last evening. Wore black frock each evening.*

## JUNE 1943

*Enjoyed Kong's talk on Chinese Customs at night.*

Kong was Angela Kong Kum Kiew who had suffered the escape from Singapore on the *Mata Hari* and even after a night on deck looked immaculate the next day in her cheongsam. She was remembered for having given a lecture on Chinese customs, which included stories about cockroach paste as a cure for fever and pounded tiger's claws for mumps. Betty Jeffrey noted the extra dimension of Kong's talk in that she missed out words. Betty said she knew them but just couldn't be bothered using them. The audience had to fill in the gaps.

Phyllis Briggs also remembered Kong and described her as being 'short with funny little sparrow legs and a broad face, always smiling unless she was in one of her moods'. For her talk, she dressed in a clean *baju* and *sarong* and wore a necklace of beautiful jade beads, perhaps the result of having a gold mine in the family. *(Warner and Sandilands)*

## JULY 1943

2 July, our thirteenth wedding anniversary. Trust you are well, my darling. Cannot be together although so well. One or two friends who know of this auspicious day were very kind to me. Kong gave a coffee party for me in the evening, and Daphne gave me a ginger cake. Marie wrote lovely verses of good wishes. Am happy in having so many thoughtful loving friends in camp.

## AUGUST 1943

Postpone Fellowship again due to coffee party given by Mrs Korinth for Queen Wilhelmina's birthday, which is wise and pleasurable to attend. Discussed the possibility of a Dutch group under Pip Myer. Held a choral society meeting to discuss plans. Norah to conduct vocal orchestral practices on Tuesdays. Myself to conduct vocal glees on Saturday. Miss D. will be our mainstay in originating harmonies. Kong plans to remove to garage 9A tomorrow. She is very unhappy and getting more mentally distressed daily.

## SEPTEMBER 1943

Unrest in camp re a prospective move. News of men leaving civvy camp for unknown destination. Many rumours. Next day, some of the men seen to leave camp on laden lorries.

Receive news we shall move tomorrow. Three households and hospital removed today. A move for the worse, being to the vacated men's camp. **Attap** roofs, living like coolies.

Hectic day moving. Travelled on a lorry full of goods with eighteen people. Not put in same dormitory as Vi and May. Am in No. 8; in **kongsi** [group] for cooking. (Three of us again. Vi and May as cooks, I am TA). Procured use of good stove, as stoves go here. There is a large square to walk in, very bad underfoot. Water problem difficult. Ate tinned beef and lunch sausage. Rations arrived late evening. Bathrooms terrible. Sloppy, squatting latrines and filthy stench, dreadful. Camp slightly better than Muntok but very bad after our Palembang camp. Dutch on one side, hospital and office. British on other side. Can see trees outside, one gorgeous high tree the colour of lilac. Rats run along **attap** in roof. Cocks live and crow under us.

*Lie on wooden boards plus our own bedding. Impossible to keep clean here, our feet are always muddy.*

Margot Turner notes the women were moving from the houses to the men's camp. But the men hadn't known the women were arriving and left the place 'in a filthy state. I'm sure they would not have left it like that if they had known.' They had thrown rubbish in the wells and left the huts in disarray. The condition of the camp was not the only problem. It was built on swampy ground and typhoid and dysentery were common.

The Charitas Hospital, run by the Dutch nuns, was closed after the Japanese found a woman carrying messages out to the camp. After this, hospitals were built in the camp and the nuns joined the prisoners.

## October 26 to November 30

*Had a good birthday on the twentieth. Coffee with the gang in the morning and evening and lovely eats. Bart gave me a delicious ginger cake containing four eggs. Oet gave me two exercise books and pencil. Pip gave an embroidered green silk case for my books and a frame. All gave flowers. Pip's dearest gift was a set of quotes for each day, and touching words of appreciation. Had four guests to tea with group: Mrs Hinch, Elizabeth, Pip and Vi. Sabine gave me a hankie; Margaret gave a set of tunes for my hymn poems. Very good of her — fine tunes. Fruit from Paddy, text from Ann.*

## November 12

*Had lovely eats in the shed amid pouring rain, it being Pip's birthday. Gave her a set of 'Thoughts for the day'. Letters have been received in camp from the civvy men at Muntok, and letters sent. No news of COJ who I am convinced is still in Palembang. One Dutch man, father of a family here, died at Muntok. Very sad for widow and children. Food has become less — when we can no longer buy from lack of funds we shall be hungry indeed. Wood is scarce so cooking is difficult. Rice, beans and* **kapal** *[fish cake] almost none. Terrible rains, bad storms.* **Attap** *roof taken off in many places, no men sent to repair it. Norah Chambers, Sister Katrina and others worked on roofs. Vocal orchestral and glee practices each week. Life mainly hard work with relaxation of sitting out at night with the gang. Getting short of money, must sell something.*

## DECEMBER 1943

December 27 – *Gave our first vocal orchestral concert. It was a great success. Norah conducted. Mrs MacLeod was soloist. This concert was repeated on New Year's Day.*

Betty Jeffrey describes the vocal orchestra: 'Norah Chambers conducts her "orchestra" in the Dutch kitchen at night. There are no musical instruments. About twenty women of all nationalities hum or ooh very softly music that has been written down from memory by Miss Dryburgh and Norah – glorious music. The orchestra is divided into firsts, seconds, thirds and fourths and all practise during the day in their four separate groups. On practice nights, they all come together and are conducted by Norah. This music is quite the most wonderful thing that has happened in this camp so far.'

The music chosen gradually grew more difficult, with Ravel's Bolero being particularly tricky. Rehearsals twice a week in the Dutch kitchen were a godsend in taking the women out of the camp mentally for an hour or two. The Japanese perhaps sensed the beneficial effect and proved difficult by sometimes cancelling rehearsals for no obvious reason. When they asked Norah to include a Japanese song and she refused, she was made to stand outside in the sun for hours. Seiki ranted that the women should not be singing while their soldiers were being killed.

Margery comments: *My thoughts are too busy with our life in Singapore two years ago. Shall be glad when these days so reminiscent of horrors are past. Now taken over by the Javanese guards* [known as Hei Hoes] *but under supervision of Hara-san and his little men. Pip gave me some brassieres, very sweet of her, and some hankies. Pip gave me white dress (uniform) and brown dress. Am very grateful as I need clothes badly now. She also gave me an exercise book, bless her, knowing I need paper.*

As well as the visits of Goh Leng, an Indian cloth merchant, Milwani, brought cheap material and thread. The women were in desperate need of clothes and even tea towels were turned into sun tops. The Japanese disapproved of the revealing sun tops but there was little else the women could do. The Japanese allowed Milwani to set up shop outside the gates to prevent a rush on his products and the women were allowed to visit him two by two.

Mavis Hannah and Elizabeth Simons went into business making straw hats out of *soempits*, the baskets in which fish were brought to camp. The customer provided the basket and paid 4/6 for the finished item.

*Sat in the shed with Pip at night and reminisced about our families. Dear old Dad, God bless you and Mother for the wonderful parents and friends you were to me. At present I buy all I can of daily food in camp, call it imperative to get what I can while I can, and not let my condition lower any more. Ann dreamed I died from a lip sore of fifteen years' standing.*

## MARCH 1944

Margery claims she arranged for news to be passed on after her death as just a practical matter but perhaps she had an intuition that if the war carried on much longer her heart would give out. She was certainly worried about her weight loss and seemed to be continually unwell. Others in the camp dying would have kept death always in mind.

*Wrote letter of appreciation of Pip in answer to hers of the twenty-fourth, and final requests to her to write to Mick, Celeste, Hobart and Syd in case I should not get through to them again in this world. Not a morbid thought, just a desire for one who knows me best and loves me to pass on news of me in case of need to those most likely to appreciate details. Awful night of storms.*

## APRIL 1944

Captain Seiki Kazue became the new camp commandant with Ah Fat his second in command. He had all the prisoners paraded in front of his table and chair, set up in the shade of the *pendopo* [hut], in groups based on their nationality. He lectured the women, with an interpreter, on Japanese military successes, which they took with a pinch of salt. Nevertheless, his assumption of a Japanese victory led him to advise the women that they would have to work hard for the men after the war because the men would be so tired. The Japanese dictated, 'No work, no food,' an order from Premier Tojo. Ah Fat was necessarily overweight, and he had a face like a pig. Seiki, in his turn, had a brutal face with a staring eye, the other eye being bloodshot and probably blind.

*Sacks of corn arrived. Was elected captain of Block 8 in succession to Mrs Woodford. Know it will not be easy to keep order and peace but must try. All public jobs are thankless.*

The job of block captain was complex and difficult, trying to satisfy people and keep the feuds under control. Jobs had to be allocated and rotated. They included rice picking, cooking, sorting out rations, cleaning out drains, chopping wood and fetching water. Often women who should have done a particular job were sick and others had to fill in. Margery felt the responsibility keenly and believed it contributed to her poor health.

*Japs weighed all of us. My weight was 63.6kgs, just after **tiffin** (8st. 5lb) so I must be 2¼ stone underweight and feel it.*

Helen Colijn noted that the Japanese authorities decided the prisoners needed to be weighed. This made the women hopeful that they would increase the rations. The prisoners were also buoyed by the injections against cholera and typhoid. Some believed that Japan was finally abiding by the Geneva Convention. Helen thought that it was more likely the guards were trying to protect their own health from an epidemic. A vendor was allowed into camp to sell food but the rations remained meagre. For a short time, the women were paid monthly so they could buy extras. There may have been other reasons too. Perhaps the Japanese saw the end coming and were afraid of being judged by their poor treatment of the prisoners, so increasing rations was in their own best interests. The takeover by the military in April seemed to improve the situation. Until then, the guards in all PoW camps had been unwanted by the fighting forces, probably country boys, mostly uneducated and parochial. Some were from Korea, others from Java, stuck in the jungle, bored and lonely. No wonder they had no interest in the women's welfare.

Shelagh Brown noted that her mother had lost 1ft. round her waist and 1ft. round her hips in the last year. Mrs Brown was now 7 stone; under half the weight she had once been.

The women were getting progressively lighter but also weaker and battling constant malaria, beriberi and assorted illnesses. They were still forced to manage the rations, cook, and clean the lavatories. On top of that the Japanese decided they should create vegetable gardens to supplement the rations. In the tropical heat and humidity, and in their weakened state, this was an arduous task. The temperature ranged from 23°C to 33°C, with humidity in the 95–100% range, day and night.

## MAY 1944

The women were on a roller coaster of misery and surprise rewards. *Unexpected arrival of chickens for camp; also sweets, biscuits. Really one cannot account for Nippon procedure after so much starvation diet. Nippon doctor says the reason British are so sick is because they are dirty.*

*Great push to show extra cleanliness to oblige this 'gentleman'. Received 2½ onions today,* **tempeh** *[fermented soya bean cake] and a little salt as extras. Last week received small piece of soap (6 cents) each, the first produced by the Nippon military since taking us over in April.*

The deaths were increasing even in Palembang although the worst was yet to come in Lubbock Linggau.

*Mary MacLennan passed away. Funeral delayed a day – disgraceful. Body in* **pendopo** *overnight. Sang the 'Homeland' as solo at Memorial service. Hectic day wood chopping, cooking, plus half a chicken – also a visit to camp of an important general, plus Mary's death. A strange and tiring day.*

Captain Seiki addressed the women, standing on a table to compensate for his stature and to add import to his message. Through an interpreter, he told them to clear out the dormitories and pack up unnecessary goods. He spoke about the possibility of Allied raids and gave the women instructions that they should gather in groups of 100 and go twenty minutes into the nearest rubber estate in that event. The firefighters had to stay in camp. They found it hard to interpret his next pronouncement that the Japanese would go with the prisoners and 'die with you if necessary'! He must have found the loud cheering somewhat puzzling.

Margery asked him whether the PoW men's camp had been told that the women were receiving 4.5 guilders per month. They hadn't but it sounded as though he would tell them. He quickly said he could give no personal message and no communication was possible because of a 'plot' discovered some time before!

## AUGUST 1944

*The latest instructions wash out Captain Seiki's previous orders. We are now required to keep quiet in case of a raid and await orders from Nippon by commandants via the block captains. And in case of absolute necessity we should be taken out to a safer place nearby. Must carry very little. Respond to orders at once and get into file in twos down the centre of camp. Hospital to go first. We should follow in Blocks headed by commandants and block captains – short walk – no turning back for more baggage. Captain responsible for members of the dorm to be there and obey orders. Four may be left to guard baggage. My life as a block captain becomes more and more complicated. Weight this month 50kg.*

One of the difficulties Margery faced was being captain of her block. Everyone's temper was wearing thin and they took it out on each other, quarrelling about following orders, or lights or water carrying.

She writes: *God knows I try to steer them and all of us out of danger, and to have such lack of support when the Nippon attitude is so grave towards us and the unexpected comes so often from them, it is a terrible danger to have insubordinates around.*

They could be slapped, beaten, tortured or even killed if they displeased the Japanese guards.

On August 22, Margery was taken ill with heart pains and was near collapse. The doctors advised her to give up the captaincy and take a rest. But no one was interested in taking her place. The other stumbling block was that the Japanese would have to give permission. The women's attention was diverted by another speech from Superintendent Seiki.

*Eventful speech by Superintendent Seiki who told us we should be moved to Muntok (Banka Island) on or before September 15, and to carry only what is necessary. It seems a very dangerous time to be moved and may never happen, but we must be prepared. Atmosphere quite electric. It means even more consternation to the Dutch than to us, as they have more children and belongings. We are allowed to send one letter per person to our homes or elsewhere up to fifty words. Shall write to Kettering [home in the UK]. Not too well today with so much excitement. Pip to see me at night for a short while.*

Part of the reorganisation involved clothes. Why Margery had a grey flannel coat in that climate was a mystery but she was sensible enough to sell both the coat and her corsets.

After her rest, Margery took over the captaincy again despite its problems. After another hungry day, she sold her gold rings to be able to buy more food. By this time, the sentimental value of their things seemed less important than keeping themselves alive. Who knew whether the war would ever end?

*Fifty big cases from the Red Cross arrived, it is said, but we have no news of contents or for whom.*

Helen Colijn reported: 'The parcels had arrived, but the guards left them outside the fence for two weeks, eating the chocolate bars and smoking the cigarettes, before they gave the parcels to the women. They contained powdered milk, sugar, canned meat, processed cheese and canned butter, all of which helped a little.'

Margery describes the women's behaviour: *Lots of nervous strain in the dormitory. Mrs Close and Joan very objectionable to me. Dixey Armstrong giggling and throwing things about. Ivy as insulting and rude as ever. Pip my dearest, most understanding confidante. Both having a financial crisis. Packing and unpacking very hard on the nerves. Having a bad time with my left ear, nostril and eye. Feels like flu. Ear deaf, so had it syringed. Felt like passing out.*

## OCTOBER 1944

*The great push was announced at tiffin time. Off to Muntok this evening, to be ready by 6 pm. All hustle and bustle.*

This camp and the short rations were not conducive to good health. Margery notes the fever and the increasing number of deaths.

*October 28 – November 19: Terrific epidemic like Japanese river fever or malignant malaria spread through the camp. High temperatures; 200 sick at a time. Hospital and convalescent ward is always full. Palembang hospital and people arrived here on November 4, final batch. Four doctors all kept busy. Big toll of deaths. Terrible feeling with so many sick and dying. The fearsome ones will go under through terror if not careful. Sang 'Homeland' at service on the nineteenth. Carried for Sammy and Plummer funerals. Pip ill with high fever, and delirious from the tenth onwards. Spent her thirty-sixth birthday in bed but was soon out again. Only gave her flowers, chillies and cigs and 'thoughts'. I thank God every day for you, Pip, you are my delightful, gracious and comforting friend.*

Margot Turner talks about the strange myth that grew with the number of deaths. She says women were turning their face to the wall in alarming numbers. 'These women usually died during the night, just before dawn. Those who witnessed their demise were often haunted by the strange tune of a tropical jungle bird that seemed to sing at their passing. The bird was eventually nicknamed "the death bird" and all manner of ghostly stories and myths were invented around this jungle creature.' *(Penny Starns)*

## MARCH 1945

March 13 – *Wrote out my list of requests in case I die while interned by Nippon. Made Mrs Hinch my executor – left most of my things and money to Pip. Hope it will never be needed – have no feeling or premonition, am just taking the precaution of getting my few things to the right people if I* do not come through, and it is impossible to save clothing and such-like for home friends when people here are crying out in need for clothes.

Feeling well. Walked with my arm on Sister's to the chair outside in the sun for fifteen minutes, very enjoyable. Glad I could walk so well after nearly five weeks in hospital and two in the Block sick. Very sad day, Mrs Penny and Mrs Blom died. Received 40g. for sale of CO's silver watch. Glad to have it to help hospital food expenses.

## APRIL 1945

*Easter Sunday.* Death of Mrs MacLeod, very sad. Molly not well.

Managed special curry eats, etc. Had nice fruit salad. Doc very offhand during the past week, sometimes rude. Today sent for me to go to the convalescent ward tomorrow as I am OK, and I am glad to go.

Removed to conv. Beginning a very heavy cold, developed more during day. Change of atmosphere good but found people very touchy.

Concerned about Gladys Young. Will do what I can for her. Trying to get sale of cigarette case and clothing as my funds are getting low. Pip is always very good to me. Went outside to be on a camp bed for half an hour. Cold still persistent, hard on the nose and hankies.

There were no further entries in Margery's diary. The camp was moved to Lubbock Linggau near Bencoolen, Sumatra, in April 1945, where Mrs Margery Jennings (Medical Auxiliary Service, Malaya) died at 9.25 am on 12 May 1945, aged 36, and was interred at Lubbock Linggau (Lubuklinggau) in South Sumatra while a prisoner under the Japanese. Her grave is marked by a wooden plank with her name burned thereon.

# *Philosophy* by Margery Jennings

*(written for Dorothy MacLeod, another of the singers,
on her birthday)*

I go my way singing
Whate'er fate be bringing
I go my way singing.
The world's my friend
O life's not for sorrow.
No trouble I'll borrow,
A fig for the morrow.
I'll sing to the end.

Betty Jeffrey notes on 26 August 1945, 'I was having a grand attack of malaria but what happened was this: A message was sent round the camp saying that Seiki would be making one of his speeches up on the hill at 3 pm. The rumours were getting stronger every hour and the excitement in the Indonesian block was terrific. They were certain the war was over. We all hoped Seiki would tell us our rumours were true, but deep down inside we thought it would be his usual rubbish.

'Nobody could be bothered going up the hill to hear Seiki, but after a while Blanche and Flo wandered up just to put in an appearance. The rest of us went on with our chores or our malaria. Getting up on his table for the last time on 26 August, Seiki made a very short speech. He announced in Malay, "*Perang habis* [the war is over]. Americano and English will be here in a few days. We are now all friends!" He did not say who won the war.'

It took a while for the news to sink in. The women were stunned. It was only when they realised they could walk outside freely and that there was no more *tenko*, no more punishments or bowing that they began to celebrate.

Allied fears the Japanese would shoot all the women were well justified and a big effort was made to find all the camps hidden on rubber estates and in the jungle. In each camp they found a list of prisoners who were going to be executed in groups by firing squad. If the Allies hadn't dropped the atom bomb, the women would have had eight days to live. The Dutch women and children suffered another danger. The Javanese nationalist movement who wanted to take back Indonesia from the Dutch were on the rampage.

In the end, 230 PoW camps were located from Burma to Java, over 3,000 miles. Rescue came for the remaining 90,000 prisoners of war and internees, engineered by RAPWI, the Recovery of Allied Prisoner of War and Internees headquartered in Singapore.

The Japanese, afraid of retribution from the Allies, started handing out Red Cross parcels and mail and even gave a concert for the prisoners to show how well treated they were. The women suddenly received medical supplies, vitamin pills, quinine and luxuries such as tea, sugar, butter, powdered milk and soap. Another gift was a roll of toilet paper (quickly called our 'victory roll') and a red lipstick, which they insisted the pasty women wear to brighten them up. Mosquito nets were handed out. Extra rations arrived daily. Men released from camp helped the women with wood cutting and hunted deer and pig to improve the diet.

While they were waiting to be airlifted out, the women were encouraged to write their experiences, which were collated with those from other camps and used in war crimes trials. Gradually through September the women were taken to Singapore and billeted at Raffles Hotel.

Margot Turner talks about the reaction of the children: 'They were so excited. They had never seen so many buildings or traffic. Some had been so very young when they came into the camp that they'd never seen a bus or anything like that. They were running around everywhere with real delight and fascination.'

Margot revelled in the comfort of Raffles – a real mattress, mirror, proper bath, sweet-smelling soap and new clothes. After a week, she embarked on the *Sobieski* for England, arriving in Liverpool on 24 October. The Home Office asked family and friends not to meet the ships. There was no official press coverage of their arrival and no central government funding for those in need. When the Japanese began reparations in 1946 a newspaper advertisement announced ex-prisoners could apply in writing to the Colonial Office to make a claim. The payment was £35, paid a year later. A brief formal acknowledgement of all the women had gone through came in a letter from George VI:

> The Queen and I bid you a very warm welcome home. Through all the great trials and sufferings which you have undergone at the hands of the Japanese, you and your comrades have been constantly in our thoughts.

# Imperial War Museum

*iwm.org.uk/collections/item/object/1030009632*

Margery Jennings' pocket diary kept between January and December 1942 and MS diary (111pp) written on pages inserted in a bible from June 1942 to April 1945 together with a transcript (113pp) of the two diaries, covering her internment at camps in Palembang (from March 1942) and at Muntok on Bangka Island off the coast of Sumatra (from October 1944), following her capture in February 1942 on Bangka Island, after she had been evacuated there from Malaya where she had been serving as a nurse with the Medical Auxiliary Service. The diary entries contain brief details of her activities, events in the camps, the food shortages and illnesses, including a major epidemic in 1944, all of which took a heavy toll on her health, while they also reflect her occasionally difficult relationships with the other internees, particularly after she was made a 'captain' of her block (April 1944), and her desperation to return to a normal life with her husband; together with a moving letter from one of her friends in the camp informing Mrs Jennings' husband, Captain Cyril Oswald Jennings, Royal Engineers, of her death in May 1945, a booklet entitled 'Poems from a Prison Camp' containing poems written by her during her internment.

# Weight loss

| | | |
|---|---|---|
| 13 August 1942 | – | Weight 58kg (9st 2lb). |
| 12 April 1944 | – | 63.6kg, just after *tiffin* (8st 5lb) so I must be 2¼ stone underweight. |
| 17 May 1944 | – | 8st 3lb (lost 3lb since last month). |
| 21 June 1944 | – | I was disgusted and dismayed to find I have lost 3.6kg in the past month (52.1, now 48.5). Am now less than I have ever been (7st 8lb). |
| 19 July 1944 | – | One kg up but think my hospital clothing is heavier than usual; now 49.6kg as against 48.5 last month. |
| 15 August 1944 | – | 50kg. |
| 20 September 1944 | – | 48.1kg (7st 1lb). Have lost 1.9kg this month. |
| 27 November 1944 | – | 46.9kg (approx. 7st 5lb). |
| 28 December 1944 | – | 44.3kg (6st 13½lb), must stop the rot somehow. |
| January 1945 | – | .2kg up on last month, now being 44.5kg. |

# Camps and Dates

1. Arrived Muntok, Banka Island, 15 February 1942.
2. Palembang, Sumatra, 2 March 1942.
3. Palembang (Dutch houses; *Bukit Besar* [big hill]), 16 March 1942 – the houses which normally held about four people were now accommodation for sixteen or twenty sleeping on the floor.
4. Palembang (next houses) House No. 2, 1 April 1942.
5. Charitas Hospital (Dutch nuns) closed after the Japanese found a woman carrying messages out to the camp. Hospitals were built in camp subsequently and the nuns joined the prisoners; September 1943.
6. Palembang (new camp), 22 September 1943 – moving to the men's camp, which they had left in a filthy state, not realising the women would be moving in. It was built on swampy ground; dysentery, malaria and typhoid were rife. Some women just turned their face to the wall and gave up.
7. Muntok (new camp), 20 October 1944.
8. Lubbock Linggau, near Bencoolen, (Belalau rubber estate) Sumatra, April 1945.

1 April 1944 – Camp Commandant, Captain Seiki [Seki] Kazue; Second in Command 'Ah Fat'. In 1948 a War Crimes Tribunal in Medan sentenced Captain Seiki [Seki] Kazue to fifteen years' imprisonment for harsh treatment of the internees.

For a fuller description of the camps for both men and women, see: muntokpeacemuseum.org/wp-content/uploads/2015/11/Camp-Dates-Revised-Final-For-Web2.pdf

# Resources

## List of the Palembang and Muntok internees of WW2:

muntokpeacemuseum.org/?page_id=380 (page 24)

## Imperial War Museum, London

JENNINGS, Mrs Margery, from Otley, Yorkshire. Wife of Cyril Oswald [Palembang PoW after escape attempt]. MAS Nurse. Sumatra internee. Died in captivity 12.5.45 [37] Lubbuk Linggau, Sumatra. Her Bible is at the IWM. (See also National Archives) muntokpeacemuseum.org/?page_id=1705

## Captivity Diaries & Resources

- Phyllis Briggs, Gordon Reis, M.J.V. Miller; Brenda MacDuff (Natural Library of Medicine, ncbi.nlm.nih.gov/pubmed/11619073); diary of W.H. McDougall, edited by Gary Topping and published as *If I get out alive* by the University of Utah Press.
- The Malayan Research Bureau Papers 1942–1945 [CO 980/217].
- The British Association of Malaya journal 1944–1973 including Red Cross internee lists and obituaries.
- British Subjects interned in Sumatra Camps May 1944 [WO208/1691] – this list contains many errors.
- The Singapore & Malayan Directory 1932, 1935, 1940.
- The *Straits Times* Archive.
- The Jeyes List compiled by J. Bennett in Changi Gaol.
- Commonwealth War Graves Register. Admiralty documents [ADM] at NA Kew. Passenger lists in the BT27 Board of Trade files at NA Kew.

## Bibliography in:

muntokpeacemuseum.org/?page_id=52

## Women's Camp Vocal Orchestra

muntokpeacemuseum.org/?page_id=387

## Women PoWs of Sumatra (1942–1945)

*Women in World History: A Biographical Encyclopaedia*

**WW2 People's War** – a comprehensive and interesting source of memoirs:
An archive of WW2 memories, written by the public, gathered by the BBC
bbc.co.uk/history/ww2peopleswar/stories/55/a7697055.shtml

**Phyllis Briggs' War** (same camp as Margery)

*Life in the Dutch Houses*

bbc.co.uk/history/ww2peopleswar/stories/22/a3550222.shtml

*More Life in the Dutch Houses*

bbc.co.uk/history/ww2peopleswar/stories/91/a3483191.shtml

**Moving Camp**

bbc.co.uk/history/ww2peopleswar/stories/66/a3507266.shtml

**Palembang 1944**

bbc.co.uk/history/ww2peopleswar/stories/40/a3502540.shtml

As for the women, over 3,000 were interned in camps in China, nearly 1,000 in Hong Kong, just over 1,000 in Singapore and over 2,000 in the American colonised Philippines. However, by far the largest group of women were the 29,000 predominantly Dutch women and their 33,000 children who were captured and interned in camps in Java and Sumatra in the Dutch East Indies (now Indonesia). Many British women and children, along with Australian nurses and other nationalities, were also captured in the Dutch East Indies after their ships were attacked during their belated evacuation attempts from Singapore.

- Malayan Volunteer Group: malayanvolunteersgroup.org.uk
- Researching FEPOW History: fepow-community.org.uk
- Captive Memories: captivememories.org.uk
- Children and Families of Far Eastern Prisoners of War: cofepow.org.uk

- Java FEPOW 1942 club; thejavafepowclub42.org
- The Second World War in Music: wo2-muziek.nl/en/
- Authorised *Tenko* TV series website (includes Muntok memorial page): tenkotv.com

## Sumatran Internment, War in South East Asia

Armstrong R, *Short Cruise on the Vyner Brooke*, George Mann, 2003.

Barber N, *A Sinister Twilight: The Fall of Singapore 1942*, Houghton Mifflin, Boston, 1968.

Caffrey K, *Out in the Midday Sun: Singapore 1941–45*, André Deutsch, London, 1974.

Callahan R, *The Worst Disaster: The Fall of Singapore*, Associated University Press, London,1977.

Campbell Hill A, *Scenes from Sumatra*. Mary Campbell Hill, 1994.

Colijn H, *Song of Survival: Women Interned*. White Cloud Press, Ashland, Oregon, 1995.

Jacobs GF, *Prelude to the Monsoon: Assignment in Sumatra*. George Mann, 1979.

Jeffrey B, *White Coolies*, Angus & Robertson, London, 1954/1997.

Jennings CO, *An Ocean Without Shores*, Hodder & Stoughton, London, 1950.

Jennings CO, *Heaven Has Curtains*. Unpublished.

Jennings R, *Memoirs*. Unpublished.

Kenny C, *Captives: Australian Army Nurses in Japanese Prison Camps*, University of Queensland Press, 1986.

MacLeod I, *I Will Sing to the End*, Coco's Publications, Worthing, 2005.

McDougall W, *By Eastern Windows*, Scribner, London, 1949.

McDougall W, *If I Get Out Alive*, University of Utah Press, 2007.

Simons, JE, *While History Passed*, William Heinemann, Melbourne, 1954.

Smyth Sir J, *The Will to Live: The Story of Dame Margot Turner*, Cassell, London, 1970.

Starns P, *Surviving Tenko: The Story of Margot Turner*, The History Press, Stroud, UK, 2010.

Topping G (Ed.), *If I Get Out Alive, World War II Letters and Diaries of William H. McDougall, Jr.*, University of Utah Press, 2007.

Tyrer N, *Stolen Childhoods: The Untold Story of the Children Interned by the Japanese in the Second World War*, Weidenfeld and Nicholson, 2011.

Warner L, and Sandilands J, *Women Beyond the Wire*, Michael Joseph/ Arrow, London, 1982/1997.

## Novels

Barber N, *Tanamera*, Hodder & Stoughton, London, 1981/2007.
Farrell JG, *The Singapore Grip*, Phoenix, London, 1978/2010.
Hardwick M, *Last Tenko* (Tenko 2), BBC, London, 1984.
Masters A, *Tenko* (Tenko 1), BBC, London, 1981.
Neville P, *The Rose of Singapore*. Monsoon, Singapore, 2006.
Shute N, *A Town Like Alice*. Vintage, London, 1950/2009.
Valery A, *Tenko Reunion* (Tenko 3), Coronet, London, 1985.

## Other

Priestner A, *Remembering Tenko*, Classic TV Press, Cambridge, 2012.

## Television

Tanamera: Lion of Singapore (1989)
Song of Survival (1985)
Tenko (1981–85)
A Town Like Alice (1981)
Women in Captivity (1979)
This Is Your Life: Dame Margot Turner (1978)

## Film

Paradise Road (1997)
A Town Like Alice (1956)
Three Came Home (1950)

## Play

Song of Survival

## Margaret Dryburgh

wikipedia.org/wiki/Margaret_Dryburgh

**Colijn, Helen** (1995). *Song of Survival: Women Interned.* Ashland, Oregon, United States: White Cloud Press. ISBN 1-883991-10-2.

encyclopedia.com/women/encyclopedias-almanacs-transcripts-and-maps/women-pows-sumatra-1942–1945

**Ager M,** (Ed.), *Song of Survival.* Song of Survival Productions, California, 1985.

## Singing to Survive

singingtosurvive.com/the-vocal-orchestra-1943–44

Margery's diary is quoted:

'However, after the third concert on 17 June 1944, recorded in Margery Jennings' diary as "not as good as before", presumably due to further weakened state of its members, the orchestra did not perform again.'

## About the Singing to Survive Concert, October 2013
singingtosurvive.com

Warner's research led to the Omnibus documentary *Women in Captivity* (1979) and thereafter to the drama series *Tenko* (1981–85), and, with John Sandilands, the seminal book on the topic, *Women Beyond the Wire* (1982).

The Captives' Hymn has been featured on *Songs of Praise*, is used at VJ Day services, and is still sung to this day by women's choirs all around the world. singingtosurvive.com/history-of-far-east-captivity/